Overcome

Anxiety

A Guide For Introvert People. Learn To Handle Negative Emotions,
Overcome Social Fear And Panic Attacks, Improve Your Conversations, Stop
Worrying And Eliminate Negative Thinking

Brandon Harris

TABLE OF CONTENTS

INTRODUCTION

Social anxiety is one of the most common psychological challenges since it affects about 5 to 7% of subjects in the general population, over a long period most often. This condition is defined by an excessive and embarrassing fear of the other's eyes in situations of simple or more formal interactions, whether in front of a group or a single person, with important consequences in terms of anticipatory anxiety and social evasion.

However, social anxiety is a mixture of anxiety and discomfort that everyone feels from time to time. For example, on the eve of an exam or presentation, it is normal to feel a little anxious. Social anxiety is, therefore, a normal reaction to potential danger. It also seems that it can increase the performance to a task (e.g. sports competition) when it is at a moderate level. On the other hand, if social anxiety affects your daily functioning and causes you significant distress, it is possible that it is related to a serious social anxiety challenges. This can cause a lot of difficulties and suffering.

When its intensity is high, social anxiety can reduce concentration, invade thoughts, cause memory and speech problems (it can be difficult to speak), almost "lose your head", even if you know that your feelings of social anxiety are exaggerated. It can become chronic, of severe intensity and cause you difficulties in your personal, social, psychological, academic, professional, daily, etc. Indeed, if the social anxiety you are feeling seems out of control and irrational, you may feel shame or embarrassment about your thoughts and anxious reactions. Social anxiety is among the most common social problems in children, adolescents and young adults.

In this book, we will discuss How to Overcome Anxiety Without Expensive Drugs such as; comprehensive understanding of social anxiety, the cognitive-behavioral approach, real-life situation; anxiety at work, anxiety in meetings, job interview, relationship, and many others.

If you are serious about Overcoming Social Anxiety Without Expensive Drugs, this book is for you to explore and have the perfect answer to your situation.

It is five o'clock in the morning, and John opens his eyes for the umpteenth time of the night. The hour is approaching. He has to give an oral presentation this morning in front of the other students of the group and his teacher. He is nauseated and unable to swallow anything. John trembles at the mere thought of going to university this morning. He is convinced that he is going to make a fool of himself and that he is heading straight for disaster.

Today is initiation day. Annie begins her university studies in a program where she does not know anyone. She hates talking about the rain and the good weather, and she fears she has nothing smart to say. Annie is afraid that it is uninteresting, and she decides not to go. Mary is in the laboratory, and her teacher watches as she does her manipulations. She feels flushed and is afraid that the latter will notice. Mary becomes more and more nervous, she begins to tremble, and she can't hide her nervousness anymore. She would like to meet anywhere except there.

These different scenarios have one thing in common: they portray people who expose themselves to the gaze and judgment of others. In one way or the other, we've all experienced this kind of situation before. But what happens when the discomfort that these situations engender invades us?

CHAPTER 1

UNDERSTANDING SOCIAL ANXIETY: ORIGIN OF SOCIAL ANXIETY

The child between eight and ten months normally presents anxious reactions if separated from the mother or in the presence of an alien adult. This is an age in which the capacities of locomotion and displacement develop, and this type of anxiety would have the function of safeguarding the excessively intrepid child.

The Origins of Social Anxiety

The safety signs are associated with the presence of the mother; the presence of a stranger activates the alert system.

Beyond this normal reaction, it has been asked whether some attitudes of the child facing new situations can already recall the phenomenon of social anxiety and therefore predict the onset of the latter in adulthood.

After several studies it has been concluded that starting from a constitutional predisposition which manifests itself from the first months of life through an accentuated reactivity towards new situations, there would appear manifestations of behavioral inhibition around the age of two years destined to evolve towards social anxiety.

One of the leading scholars in this field, Jerome Kagan of Harvard University, states that 15-20 per cent of white children is born with this predisposition to manifestations of behavioral inhibition associated with shyness; he hypothesizes a dysfunction at the level of the amygdala that would be activated in a particular way in situations of stress.

The possibility of switching from inhibited behavior to uninhibited behavior is, however, superior to the inverse one also because the predisposition to develop social anxiety tends to diminish due to the effect of acquired, educational and environmental factors.

The inheritance of social anxiety has been demonstrated: in the case of individuals suffering from social anxiety, the chances that their first-degree relative will present such discomfort are triple compared to those of the general population; moreover, if the parents are shy or anxious it is very likely that the child adopts similar behaviors.

At the origin of the disorder sometimes there may be an event that is experienced as a trauma: a humiliation suffered in front of many people, such as being mocked by comrades or taken back by the teacher at school for some reason in front of the whole class.

Sometimes it happens that it is the family that prohibits or limits to the maximum the contacts with the outside as well as to hinder visits home by friends and all this prevents the child from becoming familiar with social interactions of various kinds.

Thus, some parents, while not showing social anxiety, pass on to their children some rules that can induce in their children a certain distrust of others because they have always described them as a danger, a threat, not trustworthy or by inviting their children to pay attention to that that others might think of him and therefore take into account appearances.

Anxiety is a problem that afflicts more and more people. This is largely due to a change in society that is increasingly directed towards a model of the fast life. Starting from a concrete look at today's social context, it is possible to identify at least 3 sources of anxiety and propose 3 solutions to combat it.

Chaos and frenzy have already reached their peak in some countries, and this has led to an increase in the number of people who have problems with anxiety and panic. It is, therefore, a discomfort that is linked to the peculiarities of today's times and that in the past was not as widespread.

If you look at the life of your parents and grandparents, you can realize that the most striking change is in the different rhythm of life that marked their lives in the past. Although they did not enjoy certain comforts and conveniences that on the contrary distinguish your life today, they nevertheless lived immersed in a social context that allowed them to have more time available to process what was happening in their lives and their emotions.

This is not the case everywhere; reach some villages to find a different life trend. In some countries, life continues to run slowly, and, paradoxically, the rhythms that mark a person's day in India are very similar to those experienced in Italy a few decades ago.

At the opposite extreme are cities where this frenzy has already reached its apotheosis, where consumerism has extended to interpersonal relationships, whereby now the habit of cooking meals at home has been lost, on the other hand, the time is short, the family and relationships with loved ones take second place, in addition, to withstand stress and derived from the pressing pace of work, we help ourselves with pharmacies or intensive yoga sessions.

Even in our country something has changed and continues to change with a galloping speed, those who can't keep upstart to suffer from panic. Because something inside us requires time, time to be, looked at, lived, elaborated.

But we must realize that it is not possible to go back, it makes no sense to regret the quality of life inherent in a model of society that no longer exists. If we want to learn how to manage the discomfort caused by our lifestyle, we must first recognize this social change, accept it for what it is, trust that even in this context it is possible to feel good.

It is certainly not easy, and some believe they must choose between a working career and a family, every day we find ourselves asking ourselves what to value and what to sacrifice if time with our loved ones or our work, which is very much often as necessary as unstable and precarious. All this leads to situations of great uncertainty, where it is difficult to continue to feel good and to believe in yourself.

Even this upheaval that we find ourselves facing in the world of work clashes with our need for roots and security. The permanent contract is now history, and you are asked to adapt, to be flexible, in a nutshell, you are asked to change and give up the certainty of a secure monetary income.

As a result, everything you build on a relational level and the responsibilities you take can become a very large burden, something that slowly brings you into a state of continuous agitation and can cause a heavy crisis in your self-esteem.

How to look at this new social context in which we are inserted with greater confidence? How to stop regretting the certainties that no longer exist and start seeing this reality today as an opportunity?

Because in reality, losing certainty in something external can be a great opportunity to believe in yourself and find a center and security in something interior. But before looking at all this with different eyes, it is necessary to know what anxiety is, to accept it, to transform it.

Those who have never had an anxiety attack or panic do not know what it is and what it consists of, and so it often happens that the first attack makes you take a great fear of dying. Most people tell of their first attack, saying, "I really thought my heart would stop, and I would die."

Even if this manifestation of inner discomfort does not actually make you risk your life, you certainly find yourself having to deal with the lack of energy, with the fear that it will happen again, with the fear of being judged by others and with the sense of loneliness and inadequacy that pervades anyone who finds himself making this particular experience of physical and mental suffering.

But What Happens During a Social Anxiety Attack?

One feels a great sense of oppression in the chest, and tingling may occur in the hands and feet that announce his arrival, tachycardia and other physical pains may accompany him, some manage to cry and give vent to their state of suffering, others they succeed. Many symptoms are generalized; others are subjective and may vary depending on the person and the type of attack, which should be properly investigated thanks to an expert.

However, there are some things that can be done in parallel to try to get better, and that can help you manage this situation. Some of the most beneficial actions you can do are, in fact, deeply linked to your personal development.

Social Anxiety and Change

The state of social anxiety can be triggered by a change you are facing, and the more this is fast, sudden, unexpected, the greater the chances of reacting by becoming anxious. It can occur in professional or relational life, such as the assignment of a new job, the transition from a dependent job to entrepreneurial activity, a romantic relationship that is interrupted, contrasts with a friend or relative.

The changes that happen to us lead us to make certain thoughts, and the state of anxiety is triggered by a thought that is generated in our mind. If we can recognize it and recognize what change or situation in our life it is linked to, we can try to weaken its influence on us by interrupting it.

Why Does Social Anxiety Relate to Change?

The transformations that take place in your life take you from a state you know to an unknown state, so anything that unexpectedly takes on a new shape can scare you and make you worry.

Social Anxiety and Stress

Another factor to consider is the relationship between social anxiety states and stress. They are in fact one of the negative effects of stress, when you lead a stressful life it is much easier for you to become anxious because you find yourself overwhelmed by commitments and thoughts of all kinds, every piece that accumulates is destabilizing, and you have no time and material the inner serenity necessary to face what happens to you. The triggering situation could be something that has lasted for a long time and in which you feel trapped, with no way out, something that day after day takes your breath away and trust you.

Social Anxiety and Pre-Occupation

Social anxiety can also easily connect to the concern, which generates in us a thought that pre-occupies your mind prematurely, the concern it mainly concerns your future, concerns a fact that has not happened yet, it is going to happen, in any case, it is something that has not yet occurred. Therefore, only the projection into your head of that situation exists and, very often, it is a mental projection rich in images and negative elements that bring you into an anxious state.

We must consider that there can be a strong relationship even between social anxiety and change when something changes or is about to change we panic, and we start to feel anxious. In reality, you cannot know if the transformation that has occurred will prove to be the best thing for you in the long run.

You then create the idea inside yourself that what is happening cannot bring you anything good and will somehow compromise your future. It is a known fact that anxiety as a cognitive phenomenon originating in the prefrontal cortex in an area that has a lot to do with planning for the future.

For this reason, the person concerned about their future asks questions that lead them into an anxious condition: if something bad happens to them, if they get sick if they leave, if they predict a loved one or their job or if they become poor, and so on.

It is very important to be able to develop one's social skills in order to learn to master the various situations: thus becoming more protagonists and fewer spectators since the action leads to a decrease in the feeling of tension and stress.

Unfortunately, today, the increasingly frequent use of the telephone most especially the smartphone, the Internet and self-service shops leads to an ever-increasing avoidance of a direct comparison with the various social situations and greater isolation.

Yes, we all use the term anxiety. It is a term that is also used in psychology and medicine with very specific meanings. Although anxiety is a normal emotion, it can sometimes lead to annoying symptoms and even real anxiety disorders. Fortunately, we now know how to tackle these problems effectively.

Anxiety is a normal human emotion that we all know. But sometimes it can give problems and even give rise to real problems. The concept of anxiety has evolved by changing its meaning over time and acquiring a negative value. It was an emotion of agitation - negative or positives - associated with the anticipation of something. For example, the girl who was waiting for the beloved's return to the country could be anxious.

In German philosophy, on the other hand, there was the talk of 'angst' which means 'anguish'. The influence of Germany in psychiatry and psychopathology of the last century was enormous. The study of the discomfort of the mind started with German phenology in those lands that have become the cradle of modern psychiatry.

In the United States, on the other hand, the term - still in use - is 'anxiety' and is a strictly medical term, which indicates both the part relating to thought and the course: therefore, more clearly observable symptomatology, such as tachycardia.

The concept of anxiety in our country has evolved under the influence of German thinkers and American scientists. Nowadays, it is used to express negative emotion.

It is a normal phenomenon to feel nervous in some social conditions. For example, when you are going to an appointment, or you need to do a presentation for work. In cases like these, it is normal to have butterflies in the stomach. But if you suffer from a social anxiety disorder, every little social interaction causes you great anxiety, fear and embarrassment.

Social anxiety affects 6% of people and about 16% of adolescents aged 13 to 17 years. It is more common in females with a ratio of 2 to 1. The causes of social anxiety disorder can be traced to traumatic events, but in many cases, it is not possible to identify a single causative cause.

Social anxiety can be defeated with the right treatment. Scientific research has understood what works and what does not, setting up a specific treatment is, therefore, a must to be able to treat the problem successfully.

1.1 **What Is Social Anxiety**

Social Anxiety is an anxiety disorder, in which the characteristic fear is the belief of being watched and judged negatively in social situations or when carrying out an activity in public. What is feared most is the negative judgment of others. In general, people suffering from this disorder fear, in social and non-familiar situations, to be able to say or do embarrassing things and to be judged anxious, awkward, stupid, incompetent, strange, clumsy, weak or "crazy". The person suffering from the disorder generally has this fear when he talks to others, when he does or says something while others look at him or even simply if there is the possibility of attracting the attention of others; for example, he is afraid of being misjudged by others if they notice that he is anxious (blushes, sweats, trembles). Or he fears he can say or do something wrong or embarrassing, appears awkward, or have a panic attack (e.g. he often has thoughts like "... I will now appear clumsy, awkward ... I will begin to tremble and sweat ... others will notice, and they will laugh at me! "). Still, others may feel anxious that others may find it unpleasant or criticize their appearance.

In general, the most commonly feared situations are public speaking, going to a party, writing or signing in front of someone, making files, using the telephone in public, using public transportation. Some people fear, for example, that they have embarrassing physiological reactions (e.g. losing control of their bladder, vomiting, burping, etc.). And yet, some are more afraid of situations in which they are asked to perform, others instead of opportunities for social interaction: typical examples of this last case are expressed in situations in which the person affected by the disorder is afraid of having nothing to say or of saying something wrong, of being boring or, in any case, inadequate. These fears may be present only in some social situations or in the majority of them. However, the person who suffers from social anxiety faces such situations with extreme discomfort and anxiety, so often, to avoid such unpleasant sensations, he will begin to avoid the feared social situations in every way, with the idea that he will stay well avoiding exposure to them. The reasons for avoidance can be different: you can experience anxiety that is so intense that it is unmanageable, or you may be tired of facing situations where you struggle against your feeling of inadequacy. In some cases, avoidance can lead to a person's social isolation.

The so-called "anticipatory anxiety" is also typical : anxiety in itself has an "anticipatory" function, in the sense that it is an emotional signal that warns us, in terms of forecasting hypothesis, that one of our aims could be compromised; in fact, before facing a feared event (e.g. a student who has to take an exam) a person can experience anxiety because he repeatedly anticipates the occurrence of that event, perhaps with images of himself in which he will look bad, he will be awkward, he will seem stupid.

Images of what is feared may appear for days before having to face the dreaded event, thus increasing the level of anxiety. On some occasions, anxiety can become so intense that it hinders the subject in the performance of duties. During a meeting, for example, he may be so anxious that he is unclear about presenting concepts.

Therefore, those who suffer from social anxiety when they have a very high level of anxiety can experience poor performance. The occurrence of what one fears most usually causes further embarrassment, shame or humiliation. Thus we can establish a vicious circle that feeds the disorder, as it maintains the fear of negative judgment and anticipatory anxiety over time.

So-called " protective " behaviors represent another condition that is usually associated with "avoidance" behaviors. These are the "security measures" that the person takes to prevent anxiety from being misjudged by others. For example, if the person is at a business meeting and feels ashamed because if he takes off his jacket you will notice that he is sweating, in which case he will keep the jacket on and this protective behavior will, paradoxically, only increase sweating and therefore, consequently, embarrassment, creating a vicious circle.

Therefore, the problematic emotions most present in social anxiety are anxiety, embarrassment, the shame and a sense of humiliation; when the person is in this particular state of mind and mentality, it is even more probable that he has images of disapproval, derision, rejection or punishment of others, sometimes feeling a real terror. The fear of being judged negatively can sometimes be so strong as to be accompanied by obvious anxiety symptoms: palpitations, hand or leg tremors, sweating, gastrointestinal malaise, diarrhea, muscle tension, confusion. In the most serious cases, the fear of negative judgment can cause real panic attacks.

This disorder is quite common: scientific studies indicate that in Europe, for example, it effects on average 2.3% of the general population. Since those suffering from social anxiety hardly require help from specialists because they underestimate their problem or are ashamed, this disorder is likely even more widespread than indicated by research.

Generally, social anxiety appears more or less abruptly in adolescence, around the age of 15, after a childhood characterized by inhibition and shyness. Later it tends to remain over time, with variations in severity related to life events.

How to Understand If You Suffer from Social Anxiety

To understand if you suffer from the disorder, it is necessary to make a fundamental clarification, which also applies to all the other emotional situations, so that they are not always considered problematic. Anticipatory anxiety, embarrassment, shame, a sense of humiliation, the fear of being judged negatively and the fear of being ashamed are emotions that everyone can experience.

However, this condition does not always represent a purely clinical problem, as it could simply be a matter of simple shyness, a cause of unease, but not limiting the life of the person if it is not transformed, precisely, into an anxiety disorder. So how can a social anxiety disorder be distinguished by a condition of simple shyness or a physiological, emotional reaction?

In people who suffer from social anxiety, first of all, the emotional states are so intense and invalidating that they hinder the normal development of daily life. People who they do not suffer from Social Anxiety generally they start to worry only shortly before the start of the situation, usually, during the situation, they become less timid and anxious so that, sometimes afterwards, they will tend to care less about it.

Anxiety is therefore not overwhelming; it quickly disappears during or immediately after the end of the situation and does not lead the person to avoid it the subsequent times. Those who suffer from Social Anxiety, on the other hand, tend to worry long before the event to be addressed; it is always worse when it is in the feared situation; the next time maybe even more concerned than the last so that it could implement the behavior of avoidance or protective behavior. So, if what we call shyness or discomfort comes to lead the person to avoid social encounters or otherwise cause very intense anxiety in social situations, then we talk about real Social Anxiety.

This disorder is very disabling for the person who is affected, as it significantly limits a person's habits, compromising, in a more or less serious way, even the same autonomy, social, scholastic, or work functioning. As a result, this condition will often also affect mood due to the frustration of seeing one's life limited. Therefore, Social Anxiety lasts a long time, it could generate intense sadness, and mood drops as the person evaluate how much his life has changed after the onset of the disorder and often feels feelings of loss of hope on possible solutions.

Another condition to keep in mind, for a correct diagnosis, is that many of the symptoms present in Social Anxiety are also common to other psychological disorders. For example, the person with Social Anxiety can have panic attacks like those who suffer from Panic Attack Disorder, but the latter tend to have them in situations that are not necessarily social ones, unlike those who only experience them in social situations (Social anxiety); moreover, those who have Panic Disorder usually avoid being alone because they feel the presence of other people as reassuring; the person who suffers from Social Anxiety, on the other hand, seeks solitude because it is precisely the social situations that cause him discomfort.

Social anxiety can also be confused with Generalized Anxiety Disorder. The two disorders have in common the fear of feeling embarrassed or humiliated, but in the Generalized Anxiety Disorder, this fear is not the main concern of the individual, as instead happens in Social Anxiety. Furthermore, subjects with generalized anxiety worry about the quality of their performance on an ongoing basis, even when they are not judged, while in Social Anxiety the main reason that triggers anxiety is the judgment of others.

According to recent studies, there is no single cause of social anxiety: a set of factors contribute to the onset of the disorder, which can be genetic, psychological and environmental. As for genetic factors, they would correspond to a tendency to have anxiety reactions more easily, linked to greater reactivity and sensitivity of the nervous system.

First of all, familiarity has been found for the development of social anxiety: compared to the rest of the population, in fact, the probability of developing Social Anxiety is greater in the close relatives of those who suffer from it. Another risk factor is the presence of certain personality characteristics (psychological factors), on the development of which, once again, both genetic and environmental and educational factors affect. By personality, we mean the usual way of thinking, reacting and relating to others.

The personality characteristics most frequently reported by the same descriptions of people with social anxiety are usually sensitivity to criticism and opinions of others and refusal, the tendency to have emotional reactions, easy to worry, are often worried about having to give a good impression of himself to others, the feeling of being weak, the difficulties in being assertive, the low self-esteem and the feeling of inferiority.

Among the environmental risk factors finally, we consider the experiences in which the person felt humiliated or derided and high levels of stress linked to important life changes (e.g. work assignments that require public speaking, loss of the partner); even received family education can positively contribute to increase self-confidence and foster interpersonal relationships, or negatively reinforcing social fears.

Consequences of Social Anxiety

This disorder causes significant impairment in the quality of life in general, particularly in a series of important areas of life such as work, education, social and emotional life.

The presence of performance anxiety often causes academic difficulties. Problems in the workplace, on the other hand, are more often caused by the fear of speaking in public and the tendency to avoid commitments in which the person might feel negatively assessed, how to do work in contact with the public.

In the most serious cases, these difficulties can cause the abandonment of school or work, or lead to a state of unemployment due to the avoidance of job interviews. From the social point of view, the affective, subjects with this diagnosis are less likely to have social and emotional relationships than the general population. In the most serious cases, the person can completely isolate himself. These difficulties can also contribute to the development of feelings of frustration, sadness and a sense of dissatisfaction with oneself and one's life, or a depressive disorder, or even the abuse of drugs as an attempt to alleviate suffering. Such secondary situations further complicate the picture described.

1.2 Cognitive-Behavioral Approach

Scientific research argues that a cognitive-behavioral approach is one of the most effective treatments for the treatment of social anxiety. The cognitive-behavioral protocol for the treatment of this disorder involves the use of the following procedures:

- formulation of a therapeutic contract, which contains objectives shared by the patient and therapist and their respective tasks (e.g. homework for the patient);
- reconstruction of the history of the disorder, starting from the first episode in which it occurred, up to the detailed description of the current event;
- formulation of the disorder's functioning scheme, starting from the analysis of recent episodes during which the person experienced social anxiety;
- psychoeducational interventions, which provide information on the nature of anxiety and shame and their role in the onset and maintenance of the disorder;
- identification of dysfunctional thoughts underlying the disorder and questioning of such interpretations through specific techniques (e.g. behavioral experiments, Socratic dialogue);

- learning techniques for managing anxiety symptoms (e.g. slow breathing technique, isometric and progressive muscle relaxation, etc.);
- gradual exposure to feared and avoided thoughts and stimuli, through the use of specific techniques;
- relapse prevention interventions in the conclusion of the treatment.

This approach is applicable both individually and in groups. In the case of social anxiety, group treatment constitutes in itself exposure to what the subject fears, so it must be implemented following the preparation of the patient for it. This approach protocol can also be performed in groups.

The group approach with respect to that individual has the general advantage of enabling the comparison with other people who are suffering from the same disorder and favoring, so, the scaling of the problem and the reduction of the subjective feeling of "being abnormal". As for the exposures (effective exercises to desensitization to the anxiety-inducing stimulus), home visits at an early stage are foreseen, where necessary, in order to support the person to begin to expose themselves, to then be able to continue alone.

CHAPTER 2

ANXIETY AND REAL LIFE SITUATION

From birth, humans are exposed to dangerous situations. He reacts with fear - a condition that ranges from simple fear to sheer panic. But not in every case, this reaction makes sense. But one thing is certain: without fear, man and humanity would not be what they are.

When he does not know the chants from early childhood as "coward, pepper nose tomorrow comes the Easter Bunny and brings you rotten eggs!"? They went through the mark and leg, as one has already slipped his heart into his pants anyway. As the last one, standing on top of the high wall, one had to think twice: jump or not? Am I willing to be teased for weeks, or am I at risk of hurting myself?

In terms of evolution, one is not ashamed to be afraid of something. It made perfect sense that our ancestors, for example, had run away from a wild bear. Without fear, humanity would long ago have perished. The spectrum of things or events that people fear is individually different. Nevertheless, there are overlaps of fundamental existential fears that go back to our origins in ancient times. Fears are important as they ensure survival.

That the feeling of fear arises at all, is genetically determined. US researchers at Rutgers University in Piscataway, New Jersey, found the gene stathmin, which controls both innate and learned anxiety. In summary, the study results published by the team of Gleb Shumyatsky in the journal "Cell" in 2005 showed that mice lacking this gene were downright daredevils in their investigations.

Different areas of the brain play a role in the development of anxiety in the body. However, the emotional center of the brain, the so-called amygdala, seems to be the focal point in the development of fear according to the current state of knowledge. A fear-inducing stimulus is processed in the amygdala and sets in motion a cascade, which leads to hormonal secretions such as adrenaline, cortisol and dopamine to the fear-shaping body reactions and the after-existing fear subsequent well-being.

Tachycardia, rising blood pressure, shallow, accelerated breathing, sweating and narrowing of the pupils are some of them. Some even really shit in fear. The fear is written mostly in the face, which can be felt by extreme paleness or redness. In fear and terror, one has wide-open eyes and involuntary movements of the jaw, which sometimes even rattle the teeth. It trembles like aspen leaves because the muscles are in increased tension to react quickly. The tightness felt in the chest, and the feeling that one's throat is closed are also reflected in the origin of the word "fear".

All of these reactions go hand in hand with the actual benefit of anxiety: the extreme increase in attention and performance that the body is put into because he must react to the imminent danger lightning fast, to ensure survival. Escape or attack? Solidification or threat? In the face of an existential threat, the body is ready to perform at its best thanks to fear. With the fear in the neck, it runs, for example, faster, since breathing, circulation and perception are strongly changed and stimulated by the hormone discharge.

Sometimes anxiety does not give the body an energy boost, but even leads to its immobilization: one is then paralyzed with fear or even faints. The solidification of the salt column, however, is not the worst form of defense relative to our ancestors. Because many predators react to movement. For example, in insects or mice, the so-called fright-stiffness occurs in some dangerous situations, an involuntary dead-centering reflex with which the enemy is tricked.

In the civilized world today, existential threats rarely appear in the form of wild animals that are after us. But other fears have entered our lives. For example, stage fright or exam anxiety, which today does not save us life directly, but at best lead to an increase in performance and thus may well have positive effects for us.

Healthy Anxiety Is Right and Important

However, when anxiety leads to inhibition or morbid forms, it is naturally counterproductive. Against special fears such as the arachnophobia (fear of spiders), the claustrophobia (fear of confined spaces) or more exotic telephone phobia (phony fear) or phobophobia (fear of anxiety) as well as a long list of other pathological fears today good treatment options. In most cases, patients are confronted with their anxiety triggers in behavioral therapy and have to deal with them - do not avoid, eyes on and through is the motto.

With some fears, you learn to live, not with some. In part, our fears even haunt us to sleep. There we may run for our lives or fight with wild beasts or other adversaries. At least in the nightmares, we deal with our fears that we try to push away during the day. Sometimes they even make us a fear of death, and we wake up with sweat. Incidentally, during the dream phase, the amygdala is particularly active, suggesting that these dreams also have their origins in this brain region.

Unfortunately, children are not fearless beings. Already infants and young children are afraid, especially of possible separation from their parents and caregivers. In the course of growing up, child fears are subject to change. Children over the age of six have so-called object fears. These relate to very specific dangers. The "Top 4" are darkness, burglars, thunderstorms and animals like dogs, spiders or snakes. Behind the fears of the object hides the confrontation with their anger and aggression. Learned fear is like real fear. This is what the US researcher Andreas Olsson and his colleagues found out in a study published last March in the journal "Social Cognitive and Affective Neuroscience". So it does not matter if we have experienced certain scary situations in our bodies, or if we only know them from hearsay.

Children's negative experiences play a role in the development of fears among children. Decisive, however, is the educational enlightenment - especially by the parents. Children adapt to the fears of their parents. In terms of evolutionary evolution, this is probably one of the most important survival strategies because only those who have learned to fear situations that they have not experienced themselves.

In the course of child development, dealing with anxiety changes as children learn to recognize the feeling of fear as such. Children aged three to four start with the so-called fear-desire games, a sign that they are ready to deal with their anxiety. They have a desire to experience fear so that it dissolves again.

In their games, kids are pretty radical - for the twentieth time the plastic male - pursued by a monster of the most beastly kind - has to plummet from the edge of the table with vain cries for help and shouts of hell. Also, hiding or ghost games belong in this kind of fear. "In this game, children have only one desire - to relieve themselves. Through constant repetition of such a game, they assure themselves that they can live with their fear that can feel themselves. Fairy tales and scary stories are suitable for toddlers when they develop such imaginative games for fear processing.

Can fear and anxiety be fun too? But yes! Many people find the thrill particularly pleasurable. For from situations of defeated fear, one is relieved, freed and happy. Whether chasing a scary story or touring the rollercoaster, the hormones get going. After the climax of excitement, they reward us with comforting happiness and make no distinction between real and fictitious anxiety. Horror stories and psychological thrillers, as well as actions that put our courage to the test like parachutists or bungee jumping, will probably always find buyers. Perhaps this is because wild animals hardly hunt a man in the world today, and he must now look elsewhere for his "fear kick" and the redemptive relaxation.

2.1 Work-Related Anxiety

Isabella works for a large company, where she holds an important role. Nevertheless, she feels totally submerged by work, which gives her psychophysical symptoms of stress and conflicting emotions, leaving little room for her private life. Isabella has always had a passion for her job, but the increase in the amount of work and the change in the internal balance within the company have given rise to a mechanism already present in the background of her experiences: the fear of judgment.

In occupational medicine, work-related anxiety can be defined as the perception of imbalance felt by the worker when the demands of the work environment exceed the individual's ability to meet these demands, inevitably leading in the medium and long term to a vast spectrum of symptoms or disorders ranging from headaches, to gastrointestinal disorders, or pathologies of the nervous system (such as sleep disorders, chronic fatigue syndrome etc.) up to cases of burn-out or nervous breakdown.

The fear of being considered incapable of managing the complex work situation, of which she feels very responsible, has increased performance anxiety in Isabella:

"I answer emails at all hours of the day and night (including weekends), I am often nervous and impatient, and despite the commitment, I put into it seems that my job is never enough. When I go home to my family, things are no longer as before, and I regret that. I feel submerged."

Isabella's story shows how a particularly stressful situation at work can alter people's emotional, physical and relational balances. There are very different life stories, all of which speak of the same phenomenon: work-related anxiety. Sometimes the situation emerges from power dynamics in the workplace that put a strain on people's resilience, other times from particularly stressful moments of life.

In these and other conditions, it is important to stop for a moment to take a step back and observe the situation from the outside. Yes, ok, the situation will not be the best and many times we do not do anything to change the reality of our workplace.

What we can do is change our perspective and be more aware.

It may seem trivial to you, but by changing your perspective, you will be able to notice many things that in everyday life you "take for granted" and on which you can still act. Many times we come to accumulate a great deal of anxiety and anger, without realizing how we got there.

2.2 Family Related Anxiety

The most common group of mental disorders in the world; in some countries, while this diagnosis put less frequently than in other countries. They can take a variety of forms - from generalized anxiety disorder (a state where a person feels ongoing anxiety) to sociophobia (fear of social interaction) or fear of an object, action or situation.

Such disorders are not like the usual anxiety or excitement that periodically occurs in all people - we are talking about very strong, sometimes even paralyzing feelings. For such a condition, "serious" or even just specific reasons are not necessary: anxiety, a premonition of imminent trouble, the inability to escape from the stream of obsessive sensations can occur at any time and last for a long time.

To cope with them, however, is real: turning to a competent specialist working with modern cognitive-behavioral psychotherapy, acceptance and responsibility therapy, mindfulness techniques or narrative practices can help change a person's behavior and patterns so that he or she there was a chance to break out of the vicious circle and improve the quality of life.

Charlotte Jackson was diagnosed with anxiety and depressive disorder several years ago, but during this time she had to face not only the incompetence of doctors and the depreciation of her experience but also dismissal due to the diagnosis. She explained from her experience about how her struggle with the disorder went, and how important it was to get qualified help on time.

The first signs of anxiety and depressive disorder appeared in my sixteen years. Mom and I moved from a small military unit to a million-plus city, and at first, it was difficult. The lack of communication was especially affected: I could not make new friends, relations with my peers did not work out, and in the class, I was spread rot because I was a "nerd".

In the family, it was not customary to share experiences: each solved his problems and experienced difficulties in silence. The last two years of studying at school were not easy for me, but in the first year of the institute, everything was more or less settled. I made friends and a guy. Anxiety symptoms - a heavy mood and thoughts about the meaninglessness of existence - made themselves felt, but so far have not poisoned life.

The first serious episode of the disorder occurred in 2012, two years after I graduated from college. I had a very ordinary life, and from the outside, it might seem that everything was fine - but it was not so. Until now, I am trying to understand what was the impetus for my illness, and I can't. Most likely, it is a matter of different factors: upbringing and family, personality traits (I am a very reserved person), character traits (responsibility and perfectionism). As a child, I was a sullen and serious child, often heard from others that

I was "adult beyond my years." I don't know to whom and what I wanted to prove, but I needed to be better than everyone. Of course, this did not work out, and the understanding that comparing oneself with others was a disastrous thing came to me much later.

I constantly felt inexplicable internal tension, and even hiding my hands in my pockets, I squeezed them tightly into fists.

At first, anxiety manifested itself in dreams. Every night brought nightmares: I ran away from the angry crowd, in front of my eyes they killed relatives, I was attacked by ugly animals. To me, it seemed that something bad would definitely happen: I would get into an accident, I would go under the roof, and the air conditioner would fall on me while I was at work, the neighbours would flood the apartment, and so on.

An anxious person like me worries about the most seemingly insignificant reasons and attaches great importance to what has not happened yet - and in theory, it could be changed. For example, they send me to a press conference, and I can't sleep at night, because I worry that I can't cope with the task (although I was at such events several times), and I wind up myself, presenting the scenarios with a sad end. Imagine how (quite naturally) worried before the exam.

My feeling was connected with ordinary events: a queue at the box office, a trip by public transport, a trip to the clinic. It turns out that you live in a state of continuous stress, but "pull yourself together" does not work. All the time you're afraid of something: you think that the doctor will say that the cause of the headache is a tumor in the brain, and in the morning to the minibus where you go to work.

A sense of horror rolled over for no reason. I remember that it was my colleague's birthday, other employees (there were twenty of them) came to our office. I should crawl under the table in fear. Nothing special happened, but panic seized me: my hands were numb, my legs were shaking, I wanted to cry. Something inside me said: "Run! Runaway from here, it's dangerous!" I had to jump out of the office into the smoking-room, where I ran into plenty of bedding.

By the time I decided to ask for help, I had lost my appetite and sleep. I often cried, for a month, I lost nine kilograms. A friend worked in the neurology department, and I turned to him for a consultation. He said that I had a "neurosis" and recommended antidepressants: some cost a few amounts of cash. I started with cheap ones, and they didn't help. And then summer came, and, as they say, let me go.

I did not know that it was possible to be treated with the help of psychotherapy, and, frankly, I hardly understood what my condition was. I decided that this happens to me for the first and last time in my life. As a person, frightened by "punitive psychiatry," I thought that an official visit to a doctor would turn into a wolf ticket for me, registration and a broken career, and the drugs would bring me to the state of a vegetable.

At the end of 2012, I changed several rental apartments and work. The environment, the rhythm of life, hobbies changed, and I got an incentive - to earn money for my housing.

But in the morning, before I went to work, and returning from it, I still sobbed. Nobody humiliated or oppressed me, and it just seemed to me that I was not doing well in my duties, I was not doing everything well enough. The prospects were foggy - I worked hard and plunged into a routine.

Soon, conflicts began with a partner. I cried a lot, and she pressed on the most painful places: appearance and relations with parents. For several years, he found fault with the way I look, and unreasonably jealous - it was depressing. In addition, he had problems with work, he did not want to do anything - and I was constantly worried about how our life would turn out if, in the future, I had to earn one.

He conflicted a lot with others: he cursed with his roommates and constantly got into unpleasant situations, and this also negatively affected my emotional state. Later, I found out that people like him were called abusers, and I realized that relations with this person also contributed to the development of the disease. But I tried to cope with the experiences on my own - as a result, after two years of "emotional swing" we broke up.

I became unbearable in 2015. There were no triggers - I just completely lost interest in life and stopped eating again. The main goal of the last few years - housing - was achieved, and I did not know where to move on, I just worked hard, neglecting the holidays. And if I already resigned myself to a bad mood and anxiety, then any unpleasant things infuriated me. Everything caused irritation and anger: people, bright lights, sounds, conversations on elevated tones. I hated public transport because people in it listen to music and talk with each other - I could not be in this bank full of noise. To stop concentrating on extraneous irritants, I counted up to three hundred or five hundred in transport, hoping to get distracted. It was not possible to relax.

A friend of mine worked in a hospital and, after hearing my complaints, advised me to seek help from a specialist. The choice fell on a private medical center and a psychotherapist, about whom I read good reviews. He talked with me, prescribed antidepressants and an over-the-counter tranquilizer, telling me to come in two weeks later.

The pills did not help; the specialist spread his arms and said to drink the drugs for another two months. But I didn't notice any improvements.

After that, I decided to turn to my friend's mother, a psychiatrist, and she worked in a clinic for the treatment of alcohol addiction. Arriving there and chatting with her, I was inspired, but not for long: it all ended with the fact that they say, I am young, beautiful (only very thin), I have housing, work, and someone else is much worse. I think these words can "finish off" the patient - this only causes rejection. The doctor prescribed me an anti-anxiety medication and a modern antidepressant. Despite the fact that this treatment did not help, I am grateful to her: she noted that my condition worsened sharply, and said that if the drugs didn't work, I would need to go to a hospital.

Another month passed, and was terrible - I was one hundred per cent sure that I would live out the last days. I felt only emptiness. It was hard for me to get out of bed and go to work. I slept four to five hours a day. She sobbed when no one saw her, and even cried a couple of times in public transport. I was sure that something terrible would happen; I was about to die - I was shaking and sweating. Sometimes it seemed to me that the oxygen in the lungs was ending, and the hands were taken away. I was panicky afraid of dying in a dream and at the same time, passionately wanted this. Once, for courage, I drank half a bottle of wine and crippled myself - after this situation, I called my doctor and said that I was very ill. She recommended going to a neuropsychiatric clinic.

To get there, you need a referral from the doctor at the place of residence. I was so terrified of everything that happened to me that I did not give a damn about all my prejudices and fears of a psychiatrist. The doctor immediately suggested that I go to the hospital while replacing the drugs. I refused hospitalization, but it was getting worse.

After a couple of painful weeks, I crawled to the hospital and asked what I could do to get to the neuropsychiatric clinic. They gave me a referral, and a few days later, I ended up in the department.

I used to think that I would make a lot of money and be happy, but instead, I earned the disease.

Despite all the terrible stories about treatment in mental hospitals, I have a good impression of being in the hospital. Doctors considered me anorexic, I weighed forty-eight kilograms with a growth of one hundred and seventy centimeters and seemed to myself a plump "pie". I was forced to write down everything I eat and weigh myself every day.

A month later, I was discharged with a weight of forty-nine kilograms and terrible asthenia. I weakened, and the way to a stop or the store felt like a marathon. Then I first found out my diagnosis - mixed anxiety and depressive disorder. Previously, no one spoke directly to me about this, but the codes and statements contained the codes of the International Classification of Diseases - after checking them, I realized what was happening.

I can't say that the disease released me when I left the hospital. The treatment muffled the symptoms: poor sleep, loss of appetite, a feeling of irrational fear, and a sense of anxiety. But I did not become a happy person who lives in harmony with himself and the world around him. Imagine that your appendix has become inflamed, and the doctor gives you an anesthetic but does not prescribe an operation - the symptoms go away, but the reason remains.

After discharge, it took several months to find the drugs that will help me. And here a surprise awaited me: antidepressants synthesized in the forties, and not modern medicines, turned out to be effective for me. Within a month after the start of the intake, I realized that there was a global shift in my head. It was spring. I went to the balcony, looked around and thought: "Damn it, today is just a great day."

Medication has helped get rid of "stuck" thoughts - when you cling to a bad memory or imagine a bad situation in the future and scroll through it a hundred times in your head, driving yourself. If you draw the same analogy with the appendix, they gave me good pain medication - but I had to remove the causes of the disease myself. I began to worry less about trifles, devote more time to rest, try not to concentrate on the bad and revised my guidelines. I used to think that I would make a lot of money and be happy, but instead, I earned the disease. If the patient does not want to be cured, to change his attitude and attitude towards himself, treatment will be ineffective.

I suspect that my mother had the same disorder. Some of the symptoms that she spoke of when I complained to her about my condition, we coincided. She said that over the years, her anxiety and fear went away from her on their own, without treatment and medication. But my mother's youth was in the seventies - I suspect that then such disorders were simply not diagnosed. She has been retired for the past fifteen years, and I can say that now she has again become an extremely anxious person.

The family treated my hospitalization as a necessary measure. Mom was anxious; my father came from another city to take me to the hospital. But, unfortunately, I did not feel any moral support: my father was silent as usual, and my mother said that drinking pills were "harmful". Relatives said that I "snickered" and everything "from laziness." It was painful to hear, but I did not want to prove anything. If your toothaches, then everyone will sympathize because they know what it is. When you have an anxiety-depressive disorder, people will look with bewilderment and, at best, keep silent.

During the illness, I conceived a photo project about depression: for two years, I took pictures of myself at different periods of the illness. Then I printed a photo book and talked about it on Social Media. I can't say what inspired me to do this. Perhaps I wanted to show the world that anxiety disorders are not a whim and not a fiction, but the same serious illness as, for example, diabetes. I received mostly good comments, but as they say, the trouble came, from where they did not wait. Since I had colleagues as friends, the management soon became aware of my illness.

The head said that I did a stupid thing by writing such a post. Then he added: "I hope you understand what you are doing." We didn't raise this topic anymore, but literally two weeks later a colleague called me and announced that they wouldn't run a contract with me because of the post on social networks. When I went to the dispensary, I took the official sick leave and returned to work with the sick leave - but they fired me precisely because I publicly talked about my problems. Of course, I was hurt and hurt. I even cried. I did not understand what crime I committed in order to drive me out with shame, saying that I was "sick" and that I "needed to be treated".

Later I was told that the person who decided on my dismissal was once removed from office because of a post. Perhaps he did the same to me as he had once done to him, completed what tormented him. Now I do not write in social networks, but only do reposts of pictures and articles. I no longer want to express my thoughts and share them with others - but if I were asked to turn back the clock, I would still write this post.

I struggled with the mixed anxiety-depressive disorder for over five years - during this time, I changed four doctors, dozens of drugs lost weight, my hair fell out, I lost my job. Fortunately, my friends supported me - there were few of them, but they visited me in the hospital, and I appreciate it.

Most of all I am grateful to a friend who convinced me to see a doctor: if I didn't get help on time, everything could end sadly. My black sense of humor helped in some way: somehow, I decided that I would not settle accounts with life, because no one would come to my funeral. But in fact, most of all I didn't want to leave one mother, who, in spite of all our differences, I really love.

Now I am in remission, and I have not been taking drugs for a year now. I try not to take many things to heart, and I learn to love myself and respect my feelings. Some signs of anxiety have remained so far: I am prone to hypochondria and phobias, I'm afraid to tremble to the snowstorm on the highway, try not to walk under air conditioning and worry about the safety of my property. But all this is trifles compared to what it was before.

2.3 Anxiety in Relationship

Anxiety problems include stress, anxiety and tension. Anxiety, worry and fear to block the ability to enjoy a comfortable relationship. Anxiety can easily undermine a sense of confidence and personal power. What does it mean?

Anxiety can come mysteriously, like a sudden fog on a clear day, and it can hang for too long. The feeling can be seriously unpleasant with tightness in the pectoral muscles and an almost sickening fear. Anxiety can also interfere with work; it is definitely a feeling that most people want to get rid of as soon as possible.

However, many of the measures we take to eliminate toxic neural manifestations lead to even more problematic reactions, such as anger, depression, or addiction to a behavior. Instead of worrying, some people ignite in quick anger. Others, and especially people who are prone to embarrassment, give up what they want and experience a depressing collapse of their self-confidence and optimism but. Still, others avoid the discomfort of anxious feelings through distraction by alcohol, drugs, or obsessive-compulsive habits, such as overeating, overwork, or becoming a sexaholic or sports. These ways to reduce anxiety further reduce the likelihood that you will get the result you want.

What Causes Anxiety Problems in A Relationship?

An alarm is like a flashing yellow light that tells you: "A possible danger is ahead!" In this regard, anxiety serves important purposes as a warning mechanism.

Anxiety becomes problematic, although if instead of collecting information and creating an action plan to solve the apparent difficulty, you remain motionless. If shy blocks connect with others to find out if you want to know them more, the concern about creating relationships will only increase over time. If you feel that you cannot do something that will lead you to solve difficulties, the anxiety will linger, and more may appear. Anxiety can undermine a relationship if it blocks you from talking about issues that make you different. Are you worried about trying to discuss important relationship issues? Fortunately, the better your communication skills as a couple, the greater the likelihood that trust will replace your lack of confidence in relationship problems that need to be fixed.

Want Your Anxious Feelings to Be Even Worse?

Of course not. No one wants to worry or take actions that make the problem ahead even more threatening.

However, are you familiar with any of the following three patterns of habits? They are likely to contribute to and expand your fears, to create nervousness where no one needs it, and to ensure that anxiety continues.

Wrong Strategy # 1: Guess the thoughts and feelings of others, and then believe your guesses.

Most conjectures are based on the worst fears. Therefore, most interpretations of other thoughts and feelings of others are misinterpretations. Mind reading most of the time, comes with incorrect answers. "I know that you think that I ..." is, therefore, a useless anxious habit.

This is good news. The reality is usually milder than the worst-case scenarios that aspire and shy people consider to be true.

Jimmy was worried that this year he would not receive a promotion based on the results. His boss looked uncomfortable when they spoke the last few times, and bonus announcements were due out any day. Jimmy believed in his guesses and then fell into a deep state of depression.

Jessica believed that her husband Peter thoughtless about her than about his ex-wife. Why was he even more financially generous with his ex-wife than with her? Feeling less than in the eyes of her husband, Paulette became angry. Not wanting to aggravate the situation, scolding Peter, for treating her like a second-class citizen, Jessica emotionally moved away from him.

Exodus? Peter felt rejected. To avoid pain, when he experienced his wife as cold and unloving, he managed, stretching out his business trips. When traveling, he tended to enjoy himself, burying his suffering on long working days and the television in his hotel room at night. Jessica, however, considered that Peter's increasingly longer business trips were further evidence that her husband did not love her.

Mistake Strategy # 2: Avoid a direct relationship to the problem and the people involved.

Anxiety arises because there is a problem ahead. Therefore, alarming tension persists if there is no attempt to discuss and solve this problem.

Jimmy was afraid to discuss his problems with his employer. Maybe he worriedly suggested, sharing his fears about his merit, forcing his boss to see him even less bright.

Jessica tried to discuss with Peter her feelings about being less than in his eyes. Unfortunately, her skills to raise difficult topics were inadequate. Instead of attracting the sympathy of Peter, she inadvertently sounded accusatory, inviting a defensive line. In addition, Peter was ashamed that since he was afraid of the anger of his ex-wife, he actually often acted in a way that was overly caring and generous with her. In response to Peter's defensive counterattack, Jessica declined to discuss so that this would not lead to a fight. *Wrong Strategy # 3: Go Forward. Focusing on potential future events, rather than focusing on the present or the very next action causes problems with anxiety.*

I first learned about the dangers of what I call a "leap forward" from professional tennis players. If an athlete "jumps ahead" of the present, looking to the future to guess who will win the game, this focus on results can completely undermine his ability to remain calmly focused in the present. Is his leap ahead the expectation of victory, which made him too excited or loser, which caused a grief reaction, jumping forward into thoughts about future results, often led to a loss of the game.

The phrase in which the signals jump forward in your thoughts is "What if ...?" Another signal is the excitement. Anxiety is a generation of thoughts about possible bad things that can happen.

Jimmy woke up every morning with stomach pains. Thoughts about how his boss can reduce his bonus may also lower his salary next year, and possibly even stop his work, and he constantly occupied him.

Jessica looked ahead with Peter and saw no hope of resolving her distress. She is more and more confident that Peter does not love her now and will never be able to become such a supportive and generous husband, whom she hoped that she would get married. With these thoughts, her anxiety grew, leaving her feeling of increased tension. Fearing relief, she told Peter that she wanted to end the marriage. This felt her as the only way to inner peace.

CHAPTER 3

OVERCOME SOCIAL ANXIETY

3.1 Introduction

Millions of people around the world suffer from this devastating and traumatic condition every day. Someone accepts it as a fact, declares himself an "introvert" and makes no attempt to change anything, while someone tries to find out the cause of social anxiety because he understands how he is deprived of the opportunities that the lack of fear of communication and interaction with other people gives.

Overcoming anxiety with the courage to act seems almost a sentence made; of those thrown a little like this, like a slogan from television for a sedative; yet it is a set of words that give a great idea of how the state of anxiety is the main cause of the many blocks we live.

Life confronts us with new choices and decisions every day. Often a change of program makes our security falter, and anxiety is there in ambush, ready to launch its attack. It can be difficult to recognize profound states of anxiety immediately, and once you understand you suffer from anxiety, overcoming this emotional state requires efforts.

Social anxiety is a long-term and suppressing fear of social situations. You are subject to social anxiety if:

Be afraid of simple everyday interactions, such as meeting strangers, starting a conversation, talking on the phone.

Avoid group conversations.

You always worry when you do something that you think is awkward, which is expressed in embarrassment, blush, and sweating.

It's hard for you to do anything when other people are watching you.

Avoid eye contact.

Be afraid that someone will notice that you are nervous.

You worry that other people will blame you for expressing your opinion.

Feel the excitement and discomfort in any social situation.

Simply put, during social anxiety, a person's attention is completely shifted from the external to the internal world, and in a painful way - these are not logical thoughts, but overly emotional and irrational thoughts that determine behavior, reactions, sensations.

Social anxiety arises in different situations: meeting new people, giving public presentations, giving presentations, being in the spotlight, talking with "important" people, making phone calls, exams, parties, dating, and expressing one's opinion in a team. All these difficulties simply prevent a person from achieving his goals. For example, he may postpone a conversation with his boss for several months about an increase precisely because of social anxiety and will lose a huge amount of time.

It is not easy to cope with social anxiety, but if you follow the following tips, you can significantly correct the situation and, ultimately, overcome the problem.

3.2 Change Your Mindset by Challenging Negative Thoughts

If you suffer from constant anxiety, most likely you see the world around you as more dangerous than it really is. You are likely to overestimate the possibility of a bad outcome, immediately imagining the worst-case scenario or regarding each negative thought as a fact. You can also doubt your ability to solve problems that arise in your path, assuming that you are unstuck at the first signs of trouble. This irrational, pessimistic approach is known in psychology as a cognitive distortion.

A cognitive distortion is not based on reality, but it is difficult to get rid of. Often, it is part of the habitual way of thinking, which has come to automatism, and you ceased to notice it. You must "retrain" your brain in order to get rid of the wrong way of thinking, and as a result of feelings of anxiety and anxiety.

You should start by detailing the thoughts that frighten you: what bothers and bothers you. Then, think of your thoughts not as facts, but only as possible scenarios. Develop a habit of approaching your thoughts as hypotheses. In this case, you will learn to look more realistically and calmly at the events of your life.

Although it may seem that you are unable to do anything with the symptoms of social anxiety, there are actually many things that can help. The first step is to challenge your usual thoughts because the problem is primarily in the head.

People suffering from social anxiety have negative thoughts and beliefs that contribute to the development of fear and anxiety:

"I know that if I do this, I will look like a fool."

"My voice will begin to shake, and I will humiliate myself."

"People will think I'm stupid."

"I have nothing to say. Everyone will think I'm boring."

Combating these negative thoughts is an effective way to reduce the symptoms of social anxiety.

Step One: Identify the automatic negative thoughts that underlie your fear of social situations. For example, if you are worried about an upcoming presentation, the main negative thought might be: "I will fail the presentation. Everyone will think that I absolutely do not understand what I'm talking about."

Step Two: Analyze and dispute them. Ask yourself questions about negative thoughts: "Do I know for sure that I will fail the presentation?" Or why would people think that I'm incompetent?" Thanks to this logical assessment of negative thoughts, you can gradually replace them with more realistic and positive ones.

You also need to understand if you are using unproductive thinking styles:

Reading Thoughts: This happens when you start to guess what other people think. And even if you are mistaken in the end, usually this does not discredit this style of thinking.

Fortune telling: this is a prediction of the future and, as a rule, belief in the worst-case scenario. You simply "know" that everything will be terrible, so worry right now, although the situation has not even come and it is not a fact that it will.

Personalization: This is when you think that people think only about you, and also in a negative way.

Our thoughts form the reality in which we live. If we can change our thoughts, everything around us will change. Therefore, it is very important to be able to manage your thoughts and tune them into a positive wave. In addition to some of the steps I shared previously about challenging your negative thoughts, the following are comprehensive tips that can help defeat negative thinking.

- **Watch What You Fill Your Brain with**

Our thoughts depend on what information we run into our brain. Naturally, you may have trouble thinking if you allow the negative to enter your head every day. Therefore, it is worth giving up watching horrors on TV, news, especially criminal ones, and show shows that constantly deal with some terrible problems. Choose only creative information that inspires, gives hope, and helps you be happier.

- **Learn to Relax**

Of course, in our life, we cannot completely isolate ourselves from negative information or events. Therefore, it is important to learn how to remove psychological stress properly. For many people, alcohol is the most popular way to relax, but in fact, it only exacerbates the situation. The fact is that alcohol has a stimulating effect on our nervous system, and because of this, we become even more sensitive.

Good and safe methods of relaxation can be meditation. There are many techniques - the main thing is to choose one that is ideal for you.

- **Keep A Diary**

In order to learn to control your thoughts, you can try to write them down. Start keeping a diary and spend a small amount of time writing notes each day. In order to understand what is going on in your head, you need to see it.

If you write down every day what thoughts you have most often overcome, you can understand how to deal with them.

- **Analyze**

And do it regularly! Analyze your recorded thoughts in the diary, the actions, and events that generated them, and pay attention to how important they are. Often, negative thinking begins to develop in areas that do not matter to us. By analyzing, you can understand the reasons why bad thoughts conquer you and try to eliminate it.

- **Recover The Events of the Past**

Negative thinking is often one of the consequences of psychological trauma. For example, a guy who was abandoned and deceived by a girl now feels disappointed and thinks that all women are real evil. Recall in your memory those events when you received a psychological trauma, where you suffered, and begin to get rid of the negative experience in your memory.

How to do it?

Very simple - write everything on paper and burn it, making a firm decision to leave everything in the past and start writing a new story on a blank sheet. Of course, in some situations, this does not help - you need to visit a therapist.

- **Use Breathing Practices**

Respiratory practices today are used in many courses of psychotherapy. But, even if you do not have the opportunity to learn to breathe under the supervision of an instructor, you can do it yourself. It is advisable to practice in the open air, or with an open window so that the brain and the whole body are better saturated with oxygen.

Try to breathe air slowly, consciously gathering full lungs, so that when you breathe, your stomach rises, not your chest. Also, exhale slowly through the nose. Concentrate your thoughts only on breathing, and feel how each cell of your body is grateful to you for such nourishment. After 10-15 minutes of conscious breathing, you will feel lightness and clarity in your head, and unnecessary thoughts will disappear.

- **Connect A Sense of Humor**

Many psychotherapists recommend connecting a sense of humor to combat negative thinking. To do this, you must be prepared to recognize the negative thought or scenario that is emerging in your head and begin to develop it into some ridiculous and ridiculous situation. This exercise will help to cope with negative thinking, and will also contribute to the development of creativity and a sense of humor.

- **Communicate Less with Gloomy People**

There are people who accept their negative thinking as something natural. They like to complain about life, cynically speak about many people and things, and do not see any prospects in their life. Their pessimism is a dangerous virus that can be easily picked up. And in order not to get sick with whining, you need to stay away from chronic whiners.

- **Stop Evaluating**

From early childhood, a mechanism for determining good and bad begins to form in our heads. Subconsciously, we value all events, people, things, phenomena. But you can try to curb our subconscious. Try to live the day, not as a judge, but as a spectator. Stop evaluating everything that you see, feel, and hear. What is simply there? Do not think about whether it is good or bad - just watch.

You will see that it is so much easier not to run negative thoughts into your head, and reality seems not so gloomy.

- **Do Not Be Fascinated**

Disappointment gives rise to pain, negative thoughts, and destroys hope. You don't have to allow yourself to be fascinated, and you will surely not be disappointed. Do not expect anything from people, yourself, the world. Just live every moment, without any expectations - be thankful for the good, and do not accept the bad.

- **Laugh More Often**

Laughter is one of the best cures for all psychological problems. Therefore, try to make yourself daily no less than half an hour of laughter - it will heal your heart and help you see life from a completely different perspective. In almost every situation, there is something to laugh about, and even if not, you can laugh just like that.

Watch comedies, read jokes and jokes, communicate with fun people - all this will provide a surge of positive energy in your life. And gloomy scenarios will not occur to a laughing man.

- **There Is Something Good in Every Situation**

It's important to learn to see it. To do this, you should try just exercise. Take a blank sheet and pen, and write on paper ten bad situations that happened to you in the past. And now, in front of each, write what good came of it, or it was in those situations. Practice every time you encounter difficulties, and you will not only get rid of negative thinking but also develop stress resistance.

Probably, from time to time you encounter people who constantly complain about their problems, saying that they didn't do something or, on the contrary, did something that was not necessary and there is not always a desire to continue communicating with such a person.

It's one thing when you have to listen to a complaint from a colleague at work, and it's quite another thing to listen to such distresses from someone you don't know at all, for example, during your vacation. In the first case, you are forced, but in the second, every sane person who has no deviations in the psyche tries to stop communication as quickly as possible.

So, you did not think, why exactly do you have a desire not to listen to other people's complaints?

How to Stop Constantly Thinking About the Negative?

Whining and other people's problems are of little interest to anyone, and in most cases, if there are any problems, then you need to solve them. A man is the blacksmith of his life, and if there are any questions, you need to solve them yourself, because no one will help a person better than himself.

If you constantly scroll through your problems, this leads to the fact that the negative accumulates and as a result, it climbs sideways in the form of diseases. If you do not want to be treated later, prevent future illnesses mentally, that is, stop thinking about insoluble situations, and just solve them.

In order to get rid of the discomfort within yourself, while not deciding the cause of the discomfort itself, you can simply pronounce it whether it is important whether it is a girlfriend, a stranger or just walls. This method (it is not effective) of temporarily getting rid of spiritual discomfort is beneficial only to the individual himself, but the problem remains a problem, while the person to whom you have entrusted your adversities will, in any case, have an opinion about you that will be constantly designed, whether he wants it or no.

Dissatisfaction with oneself and life can become the reason that a person himself, not noticing it, begins to spoil life for himself and his associates, and the time that could be spent on solving a specific problem is wasted on talking.

If you see that the person with whom you decided to speak out is trying to get away from the conversation and he has a displeased face, it means you are doing something wrong and now the question arises, was it worth it to start the conversation? Of course, the interlocutor may have many reasons for the displeased person, but you don't need to be selfish and constantly talk about your sorrows, because a normal person constantly listening to pity will begin to get bored, and in general will lose interest and will eventually try to evade the conversation as such for some reason completely.

People more like to listen to positive information, and the point is not even flattery, but the fact that while listening to positive information, even the mood improves, and it's much more pleasant to communicate with a person who is positive, than with a whiner.

As a result, some people try to calm themselves down while talking about a problem, but without solving it, while others, on the contrary, act and get rid of it, it turns out that talking in vain does not lead to anything, they only give a soothing effect for a while and do no more, therefore, "speaking the problem" is not a method of solving it and it is not true.

So, how to find your way to solve problematic issues in life? Alas, there are no universal options, because each case is individual, but there is an interesting algorithm of actions, listening to which you can bring yourself closer to the goal. The first thing to do is to compose for yourself in your mind or write down on a piece of paper several ways to resolve a controversial situation.

If you didn't manage to solve the problem, try to find more ways to solve it, if it is half solved, then this is the result, you tried, but if you find out everything for yourself and get a negative or positive answer, you can be calm, because it's is there a result.

So, your problem has remained in the past, and you begin to spend your time and health vigorously on thinking this kind: "what would happen if" and so on. It is necessary to stop because such self-digging will not lead to anything; history is already in the past; we must think about the future and act. Engage in physical labor, and it will distract you and bring its results, well, and ultimately cheer up.

Learn to see yourself from the outside, developing a high level of self-control, because only in this case you will stop digging in the past and think about the negative. Life energy does not need to be wasted thinking about what would happen if it is very destructive. You need to tune in to positive, even if the negative does not come out of your head, find something good around you and make it the center of your thoughts.

In order not to destroy yourself from the inside, tune in to positive thinking, because you must have the instinct of self-preservation.

The internal state of a person depends solely on him, so you need to concentrate on the positive. You managed to set yourself up for positive, but what if people with negative surround you? Yes, there are situations when you can't escape from negativity, but if you learn to develop a positive attitude (if you haven't developed it since childhood), you can minimize the negative that you get from talking with him.

People who think about the bad have always been and will be, and this is a given and should be treated calmly (unless, of course, you have the strength to listen to something negative constantly) and let all of this pass by. To think positively, you need to work a lot and hard on yourself, both emotionally and physically, while often overdoing laziness.

Negative information is completely useless; it is destructive and destroys, so you need to make sure that it passes by you. If you cannot listen to your negatively minded interlocutor, limit the time and opportunity to communicate with one and hint to him subtly that you are more interested in other topics for conversation. Bring the interlocutor the thought at an abstract level that bad thoughts are reflected in real life and are the cause of failure.

If you want to help your interlocutor, offer several options for solving his situation and if he ignores your recommendations just transfer the conversation to another topic, as it is clear that the person is not interested in solving the problem, but simply wants to complain and thereby calm himself, and we know that such conversations do not lead to anything.

So, we draw conclusions, to stop thinking about the negative you need: Regularly work on yourself, while trying as little as possible to concentrate on the negative, think about the good. It is not necessary to focus attention on negative situations in your life and try to quickly forget all this, while clearly understanding that thinking about the negative can harm your body.

A positive attitude is an essential companion of an active lifestyle. If a problem has arisen, it is necessary to clearly and quickly accept it as it is and to realize it, outline an action plan for its elimination, proceed with its implementation, while not forgetting to spend at least 2 hours a day in the fresh air, and also enter into your daily routine, start doing gymnastics or any other physical exercises.

Have You Had to Deal with Negative People?

If yes, then you know that it can be difficult. I recall my former colleague, who was just like that. During our conversations, she endlessly complained about colleagues, about work, and about life.

However, she spoke very cynically about people in general, constantly doubting their intentions. Talking to her was not a pleasure. Absolutely. After our first conversation, I felt completely exhausted. Although we talked for only 20-30 minutes, I had neither the mood nor the strength to do something else.

There was a feeling that someone had sucked my life out of me, and it took about three hours for this effect to pass. When we talked later, the same thing happened. She was so pessimistic that her negative energy seemed to pass on to me after the conversation and even left an unpleasant aftertaste in her mouth.

And you know, it bothered me a lot. I would gladly refuse to communicate with her if I could. Then one day, I decided that I needed to develop an action plan - how to deal with negative people. In the end, she is not the only person I meet in my life. I thought: For every negative person I meet now, there will be thousands of those whom I can meet one day. If I learn to cope with it, I can cope with everyone else.

Keeping this in mind, I brainstormed on how best to deal with negative people. In the end, I found a few key tricks to do this effectively. They can be very useful to build good relationships with such people. And although now I deal more often with positive people, these steps come to the rescue when I sometimes meet negative people.

If there is such a negative person in your life now, you do not have to suffer from it. You are not alone in your problem - I often encountered negative people and learned how to deal with them. Let them try to lower you - you can choose how to react and what to do.

So, these tricks work for me, and certainly, it can also work for you to help you deal with negative people.

- **Do Not Let Yourself Get Negated**

I noticed one thing negative people tend to focus on bad things and ignore good ones. They exaggerate the problems they face, and therefore their situation seems much worse than they really are. The first time you communicate with a negative person, listen carefully, and offer help if necessary. Provide support - let him (she) know that he is not alone.

However, make a mark somewhere. If a person continues to complain about the same problem even after several discussions, this is a sign that you need to free yourself. To get started, try changing the subject. If he (she) goes into a negative corkscrew, let him (her) continue, but do not get involved in the negative.

Give simple answers like "Yes, I see," or "Yeah." When he (she) will respond positively, respond in the affirmative, and enthusiastic. If you do this often enough, he (she) will soon understand what is happening and become more positive in communication.

- **Use Groups Talking with A Negative Person**

When I talked with my negative colleague, I was completely exhausted for several hours, although the conversation itself lasted only 20-30 minutes. This was because I took on all of her negativity. To solve this problem, let someone else be with you when you are talking with a negative person.

In fact, the more people, the better. Then the negative energy will be shared between you and other people, and you will not have to bear its severity alone. An additional plus from the fact that someone else will be nearby - other people help to identify different sides of the individual.

When there are others nearby, they can help discover a different, positive side of the negative person. I had experienced this before, and it helped me see the "negative" personality in a more positive light.

- **Objectify Comments Negative People Can Be Quite Critical at Times**

They periodically release comments that can hurt very much, especially when directed at you. For example, I had a girlfriend who was very tactless. She loved to give out various dismissive and critical comments. At first, I was worried about her words, wondering why she was so critical every time she spoke.

I also thought maybe something is wrong with me - maybe I'm not good enough. However, when I watched her communicate with our mutual friends, I realized that she behaves the same way with them. Her comments were not personal attacks - this was her usual behavior.

Recognize that a negative person usually does not want to hurt you - he or she is simply trapped in their own negative. Learn to deal with negative comments. Objectify them. Instead of taking his (her) words personally, consider them as another point of view.

Drop the husk and see if you can benefit or learn from what is said.

- **Switch to More Pleasant Topics Some Negative People Start-Up On Certain Topics.**

For example, one friend turns into a "victim of circumstances" whenever it comes to work. No matter what I say, he will continue to complain about a job where everything is just awful and will not be able to stop. If a person is deeply rooted in his negativity, in his problems, a change of topic may be the solution.

Start a new theme to cheer you up. Simple things - movies, daily incidents, mutual friends, hobbies, happy news can greatly facilitate the conversation. Support him in areas in which a person experiences positive emotions.

Carefully Choose with Whom You Spend Your Time

You are the typical person of the kind of people you spend the most time with. This words of wisdom mean that those with whom you spend time have a huge impact on how you become a person. I think this is very true. Think about the time you spend with negative people - do you feel good or bad after that? The same thing with positive people.

What's that feeling like after spending time with them? Whenever I spend time with negative people, I feel heavy after that, and I feel a bad aftertaste. When I meet positive people, I feel a surge of optimism and energy. This effect remains after communication. By spending more time with negative people, you gradually become negative too.

At first, it may be temporary, but over time, the effect will begin to take root in you. If you feel that certain people in your life are negative, realize how much time you spend with them. I advise you to limit the duration - this can help. For example, if they want to chat with you, but you don't like their company, learn to say no.

If it is a meeting or a phone call, set a limit on how long they will last. Stick to the topic of discussion, and do not let it last longer than a certain time.

- **Identify Areas in Which You Can Make a Positive Difference**

Negative people are negative because they lack love, positive, and warmth. Often they behave in such a way as to create a barrier that will protect them from the world. One of the best ways to help them is to bring positive things to their lives. Think about what is bothering the person now, and think about how you can help him (her).

This should not be too complicated, and you should definitely not do this if you do not want to. The key is to be sincere in the desire to help and to show him (her) a different outlook on life. Some time ago, I had a girlfriend who did not like her work. She did not like the environment and corporate culture. A vacancy appeared at my (already former) workplace, so I offered her this opportunity.

She eventually got this job, has been doing it for 3 years, and she is doing it perfectly. Today she leads a much happier, more active, and optimistic life. She is definitely more positive than a few years ago. Although I have not yet bet that she will be completely happy with her career, I feel satisfied that I helped a little at the right time.

Besides, there is always something that you can help another - look around and help with what you can. A small action on your part can lead to big changes in your relationship.

- **Stop Talking to Them If All Fails**

Limit contact with these people or even completely remove them from your life. Instead of spending your time with negative people, focus better on positive people. Previously, I spent most of my time with negative people trying to help them. It took me a lot of energy and was often completely useless. I revised my methods. Now I prefer to work with positive friends and business partners. It turned out to be both more pleasant and more useful. Remember that you are building your life, and you decide what you want it to be. If negative people make you feel bad, work on it using these steps outlined. By acting correctly, you can noticeably change your relationship. Pay attention to your body when negative emotions grip you. Look at your face: the corners of the mouth are down; the forehead is frowning.

How do you hold your back? Slouch? If you have a hotbed of negative thoughts in your head, the body behaves accordingly. And when such thoughts become permanent, it gets used to such a situation. You probably saw people with a mask of contempt or anger on their faces, which persists in any situation.

This also works in the opposite direction: the pinched position of the body and the frowning face create not the best mood. So, your first step in getting rid of bad thoughts will be a change in posture and facial expression. Straighten your back and straighten your shoulders.

Feel where the tension has accumulated in the body, and relax, smile. In just a few moments, you will feel that the emotional background is changing.

- **Discuss Your Feelings**

Some people tell everyone in a row about their problems and even relish it. Others keep everything in themselves to the last, and then they get a nervous breakdown.

If you still have any negative emotions that do not go away, try to tell loved ones about it. Putting on words, you give emotions a form and see them in the right perspective. After the conversation, you will be surprised how stupid it was to worry about the voiced issue, and the negative will disappear.

- **Stop The Flow of Thoughts**

If a thousand thoughts rush through your head in one minute, it's hard to decide something for yourself and at least somehow control it. If you hang on the negative, try just one minute to not think about anything at all. Paying attention to what is happening in the head and what thoughts dominate there, you can change the situation.

Change the wording. It is amazing how the tone of a whole phrase or thought changes from a small change in wording.

Compare: I have a difficult period in my life, I have problems, and I have a period of changes in my life, I'm looking for the best solutions. The source data has not changed, just the problems called changes. But who will say that this is not true?

Get creative when negative thoughts attack you; you can spend a little time on creativity.

It works just like a conversation, with the exception that you don't have to get anyone with your problems. You can do anything: write prose or poetry, draw with a pencil or paints. A splash of emotions through creativity is a kind of art therapy, which will not only provide relaxation but also cheer up.

Negative thoughts will pass through you, become embodied in the form and remain in it, and not in your head.

- **Take A Walk It Often Seems That Our Head Is the Only Source of Negativity**

Most often, it is, but it happens differently. If toxic people surround you, for example, in a family where everyone quarrels and blames each other, or at work, where everything is on the nerves, half of the negative can be due to their mood.

If you are not a guru, it is unlikely that you will be able to get rid of heavy thoughts while being in such an environment. Therefore, if possible, leave it to calm down. Go for a walk or go somewhere: to the exhibition, to your favorite cafe, to the cinema - this will help you find it.

- **Make A List of Thanks**

Sometimes we forget about all the good things in our lives. It seems that there is no way out and on all fronts a complete failure. So, sitting in a cozy and warm apartment, having come from his beloved job, a person may think that his life is a cesspool, and he is a complete loser. And all because of the coincidence of minor troubles in a day or an unfinished project hanging over the soul.

To cope with this condition, write down everything good that is in your life, what you are for. For example, I am grateful for my appearance and health, and I am grateful for loving and beloved relatives, I am grateful for true friends. Look at the resulting list and see for yourself: minor troubles cannot outweigh this.

Negative thoughts are those thoughts that are related to other people, to yourself and the world around us. They involuntarily appear in our consciousness, as a rule, are irrational and make us feel bad. How to identify them? These are generalizations: when a thought contains words such as nothing, everything, never, always and makes you feel bad, think about it.

These are thoughts in a dramatic spirit: This is terrible, disgusting, there is nothing worse than. Predictions of the future: I will fail. We are trying to get ahead of events as if we knew in advance what would happen. Admitting guilty of everything: My colleague was too rude with me, I am sure that it is my fault. Ability to read the thoughts of other people: I did not say hello to him, I am sure that he considers me a boor.

- **Record Your Negative Thoughts**

The first step to getting rid of negative thinking is to realize the negative thoughts that visit us throughout the day. If we are aware of their existence, and why they arise, we will be more prepared to analyze and change them.

How to do it?

Keeping a list of habitual negative thoughts that you want to get rid of is a very effective way to learn this. Always carry a notebook or piece of paper and a pen. You can record not only the thought that visited you but also more detailed information about it.

For example, to describe the feeling of discomfort that it caused you, what exactly made this thought appear in your mind, and what you did later.

Find an alternative to negative thoughts. After you write down some negative thoughts, they will become more conscious for you. And then you will understand that it is precisely these thoughts that you call realistic that make you feel bad. Come up with an alternative to them.

How to do it?

If, for example, you thought: This interview will be a disaster, I won't be able to pass it, I'm not qualified enough for this, you can change this idea as follows: Perhaps I am not an ideal candidate for this position, but I will do everything possible to show myself well at the interview. You can write down alternative thoughts in your notebook.

Gradually, with experience, alternatives will come to your mind by themselves.

Do not try to read other people's thoughts; many negative thoughts visit us because we are trying to guess the thoughts of other people. We think we know what others are thinking. For example, if we notice that a colleague did not suddenly say hello, we might think: This is because he does not like me. Are you, by any chance, not a telepath? In truth, no one has yet demonstrated this ability.

How to do it?

Since we know that you are not a telepath, think about objective facts. Act like a scientist. Ask yourself: Do I have any evidence that this is so? Does science confirm that my colleague does not like me? Or did he tell me about this himself?

Regardless of whether you have evidence or not, but you still think that a colleague does not like you, why don't you check it by asking him directly? If you cannot obtain objective data, you do not have sufficient evidence that this is so.

Therefore, come up with an alternative explanation for yourself that will not cause you such discomfort: Most likely, he did not notice me or his day simply did not work out. You can make a list of the most likely explanations for each similar situation.

As previously identified, you can throw negative thoughts into the trash. As a result of a study at Ohio State University, with the assistance of researchers from the Autonomous University of Madrid, it was found that writing negative thoughts on paper and then crumpling and throwing this paper in the trash helps us get rid of the negative.

This mechanism helps to designate a negative thought as an unnecessary, useless object, like garbage.

How to do it?

It's not hard. Just write negative thoughts on a piece of paper that you would like to get rid of. Crumple or tear this piece of paper into pieces and throw it in the trash. This mechanism also works if you do this using your computer: write your thoughts in a text editor, and then drag the document into the trash.

If you don't have any of this at hand, you can try to visualize your thoughts and throw them into an imaginary trash can. It is possible that your thought will return again. In this case, you can try to do the same again. With time and practice, your negative thoughts will take longer to return.

- **Surround Yourself with Positive People**

How to do it?

Try to spend as little time as possible with "toxic" people who infect you with their negatives. Spend more time with positive people. Learn from them to see the world in a positive light and ask for advice. When you have a negative thought, ask them what they think about it. How to stop thinking negatively: surround yourself with positive people

Enjoy the good things quite often, and our negative thinking is based on the inability to enjoy those positive moments that happen in our lives.

How to do it?

Do not underestimate your achievements; praise yourself for them. Learn to enjoy the present. Mindfulness meditation practice can help you with this.

Do not complain too much Complain about misfortunes is sometimes useful because, at a certain point, it helps to let off steam. However, when we constantly complain, we again focus on negative thinking. And besides, we are not doing anything in order to correct a situation that does not give us rest.

How to do it?

Whenever an unpleasant situation arises, and there is a desire to complain, first think: Can this be somehow settled? Is there a solution to this problem? If a solution exists, do not waste time complaining and resolve the problem. If the problem is unsolvable, try to see the situation in the best way. Accept it.

Mindfulness meditation can also help us accept the unpleasant things that happen in our lives. No situation, positive or negative, lasts forever. They are like clouds that come and go.

Do not generalize negative experiences Are you one of those who say: this always happens to me, what a loser I am? Summarizing the negative that is happening to you, you not only feel worse but also see the situation far from what it really is.

How to do it?

When you think or say things like it always happen to me or everything bad happens to me, stop for a moment and think. Is this really so? Make a list of the good things that happened to you in life. Thanks to this, you will see that this is not so, and not only bad things happen in your life. Of course, negative experiences are inevitable, and setbacks do happen. But we also experience wonderful moments, which sometimes we do not pay due attention to.

3.3 Change Your Habit

We all do a huge amount of things out of habit. Thus, our system saves us energy. Just imagine what would happen if we thought about how to brush our teeth every time, or when to brush them, etc.

Some habits help us out, they help us work more productively, or simply make our lives easier. They give us the opportunity not to think every time on the same action, because it turns into an automatic task. We can call them useful, and they include such habits as going to bed at a certain time, getting up early in the morning, the habit of finishing the job to the end, the habit of achieving the task, etc.

On the other hand, there are habits that, frankly, spoil our health, well-being, and, ultimately, our whole life. We can classify such bad habits as seizing stress, smoking, scattering things, putting off important things, overeating, etc.

And we all want to replace our bad habits with good ones. However, we depend on habit, because we carry out the action completely thoughtlessly, the subconscious is responsible for this, and it reacts thousands of times faster than consciousness. That is why it is so difficult for us to change a habit because our mind is late. Thus, in order to start changing a habit, we need to begin to notice our pattern of actions, to perform an action consciously and constantly to control ourselves, and this is not so simple. Slouching, for example, is a very bad habit common to many.

If a person sees himself in the mirror, then he immediately tries to straighten himself, but after a second he returns to his pattern and continues to stoop. So what to do? It is known that one cannot completely get rid of a habit; it can only be replaced by another. And for this, it is necessary to understand how a habit is created, disassemble it into its components and study what mechanism triggers the action of the habit.

Perhaps you, too, could notice how much in our life we live the same days. The same days add up to the same weeks, which neatly fit into the same months. We wake up with the same mood every morning. Every day we live with the same set of thoughts and actions. We even want the same day after day.

Nothing changes.

On the one hand, it's even good. Without unnecessary mockery, I will say that in this situation, stability and order reign in life. It has long been known what can be expected from life and what to do about it.

Surprisingly, this is good from the point of view of conservation of strength and energy. After all, a person in such a lifestyle and rhythm absolutely does not need to invent a new behavior, vision, presentation, form a different or broader worldview, change, in a word. Everything happens automatically. No stress.

Yes, even the brain is so arranged! Any of our response to what is happening is based on experience. It is economical and fast. A person does not need to come up with a new reaction every time. Everything happens in an elementary way: a situation happens that is compared with experience, then a similar case is found, and on-the-go gives a ready-made answer.

So a man gets trapped like a squirrel in a wheel repeating the past over and over again. This is how habits, behavioral, and mental stereotypes are formed. So a person deprives himself of another future.

In fact, everything that a person develops, collapses, is present or absent in life, is connected with what stereotypes and habits he uses. Problems begin only when a person once, suddenly, by accident, wants to or begins to feel that he needs something else, something that does not fit into the framework of his life today.

Oh, it's terrible when you suddenly realize that with all your abilities and talents, you are persistently doing something, which further immerses you in the swamp. And what to do differently, you still do not know.

And after a while, you realize that you need to learn something anew, in a new way, in a different way. We have to change, change a lot of what I thought you know how to. It is necessary to transform from a person who lives exclusively as a hackneyed record, endlessly repeating his past, into a person who chooses the future. It chooses, because, with a habit, nothing can be done but to realize it, to see. And then you can make your choice - either follow it or find another option.

On the one hand, these are all common truths. But why are there so many people who prefer not to change anything? There can be many real reasons. Among them, there are very not flattering. But I still explain this to myself because of the lack of tools. A person does not know how to go beyond his stereotypes.

Therefore, today, I want to give a couple of simple techniques and tools that will allow you to independently shape your life by throwing in yourself such a garbage bin that has long been obsolete.

And as always, you need to start from the very beginning, which, at times, is the most difficult moment along the way. You really need to be more patient and have a little faith in yourself. And ask yourself a couple of questions:

What Does Not Match Me?

Not in others - in oneself. It can be anything, and the habit of smoking, and arrogance, and the habit of arguing, anxiety, depreciate yourself, etc. If suddenly it turns out that you are just very happy with yourself and you are happy with everything, this also happens (!), but here the "others" interfere with a full-fledged life, then answer another question:

How Does This Relate to Me?

Well, for example, you are all a beautiful perfect woman, and all men are goats. This fact must be very frustrating! And still ask yourself the question: what am I doing, that all men turn to me with their goat side? And by analogy, a number of other questions: What am I doing, what do not value me (everyone is dissatisfied with me, letting me shout at me, etc.)? Depending on what excites you. *When a clear concrete answer is received to the first question, we can safely move on:*

How Would You Want to Be Otherwise?

It is not superfluous to recall that your description should be positive, i.e., you easily and selflessly and delightfully describe what you think may be present in your life. For example, instead of smoking - a calm attitude towards cigarettes, instead of envy - joy for another.

Try to imagine a holistic image of your new behavior or feeling, with all the nuances that accompany it. Include in it not only what you do differently, but how you feel. How differently in connection with your new choice, events unfold, what situations are developing, even what people appear in your life. In such a simple way, you begin to form a new habit. Therefore, feel free to draw any details that are acceptable to you. This is your image! Any habit is imprinted in our brains by means of strong emotions or repeated repetition. This fact cannot be neglected by us either. Try to ensure that your image is filled with positive emotions and impressions, so you bring the emotional component.

Well, of course, do not forget about it right away, as you created it. I won't deceive you, but it takes time to redirect yourself and turn yourself one hundred and eighty degrees. Do not be too lazy to find it for yourself. You only need 10 minutes before bedtime, so that when you lie comfortably on a pillow and nobody and nothing bothers you, close your eyes and live in this new view, in the truest sense of the word, getting used to a new image, a new life direction. And after a while, you won't even notice how gradually, easily and naturally everything starts to change.

In the arsenal of psychologists, thousands, just thousands of techniques to help realize any behavior, form any attitude, and create any habit. And still, do not forget that a person is not a computer! Any program you can't put into it! Therefore, the image that you began to form should correspond to your values and priorities.

And yet, this is only the beginning, which may seem like an amazing adventure, when a person suddenly ceases to be dependent on the conditions that created him and begins to choose his path. And I wish you faith and ease when you create your life scenario.

Now you know how to change your habits and lifestyle. Give it a try. Observe your habits, calculate triggers to understand your weaknesses, and where to put more effort. Understand which reward you prefer, are you ready to give up momentary pleasures for the sake of something more? Keep mindful and, most importantly, enjoy what you do or what you do it for.

3.4 Reducing Shyness

Shyness is a periodic state of the psyche caused by a combination of external factors and internal sense of self, manifested by behavioral reactions and is characteristic of both humans and animals. Shyness includes a whole set of traits that together form this character trait.

These include tension, timidity, insecurity against the background of a lack of social and communication skills, a certain degree of awkwardness in social interaction.

The reasons for shyness always lie in the desire to hide his true identity because of the fear of interaction, so a person is quite accurate in his statements and manifestations. Because of this style of behavior, shyness is often mistaken for inner modesty, refinement, restraint, secular manners, but at the same time it is not an external reflection of the presence of these qualities, it is only a mask that looks like this.

Do not worry if you periodically feel awkward in this or that situation. This is completely normal; it is just necessary when shyness begins to affect normal life. Self-doubt, excessive timidity, and indecision - these are not the best assistants in building relationships or moving up the career ladder.

In some cases, these traits of our character can simply poison our lives. To prevent this from happening, let's talk about the causes of shyness and what needs to be done to get rid of it.

What is shyness, and where does it come from?

Why do a certain number of people feel comfortable in any situation, and for some, communication with the opposite sex, colleagues, public speaking, and much more cause unpleasant, even painful sensations? Perhaps it is all about excessive self-criticism.

A shy person suffers from self-doubt, as well as from low self-esteem. They are ready to abandon a promising position, romantic relationships, so as not to stand out from the crowd and not attract attention to themselves. Modern psychologists define shyness as a mental state, which is characterized by:

- stiffness
- indecision;
- fearfulness;
- social awkwardness;

Shyness

They usually appear as a result of a lack of certain social skills or self-doubt. It is very dangerous that those around them are often characterized as modest, restrained, and balanced. Unfortunately, such an opinion can do a disservice.

Let me give you a good example. Teachers of the old formation brought up on values, often put children whose character is inherent in the above qualities, as an example to everyone else. Result? A person grows up and develops with the understanding that he has chosen the right path.

Going beyond the threshold of the school, he tries to stick to the wound of his chosen manner of behavior. What is it facing? Of course, with a misunderstanding. And then more. Closure, complexes, and everything else. Naturally, there are such shots that are capable of enchantingly playing in public. But they don't interest us, and we are talking about those people who are shy are really trying to hide.

They are ready to get rid of friends if only to reduce the impact of stress that they experience in communication. Have you noticed that your loved one is lost when communicating with sales consultants, or are very nervous if they have to make a phone call to a stranger? Do not disregard this.

Such people really need professional help. I don't want to scare, but if I don't react to such cases, the situation will only get worse. In the soul of such people, there lives a small but voracious "worm" that slowly but surely eats up self-confidence. Do not expect that a person will be able to overcome this condition himself. I can assure you that for him this is tantamount to a feat.

So where does it come from, this destructive modesty and shyness? Ready to name a few main reasons:

- attitudes acquired in childhood regarding the framework of public decency;

- lack of social skills necessary for a normal existence in society;
- the person's confidence that he is shy (can be "vaccinated" by parents or teachers, or be his conclusion);
- genetic predisposition.

According to neurobiologists, excessive shyness causes difficulties in the work of the brain (the exchange of neuronal neurotransmitters) and a number of other problems. You need to get rid of shyness. Otherwise, it will simply poison your life. What do I need to do? Let's talk about this further.

How to Get Rid of Shyness?
Shyness: A Few Steps Towards Deliverance

Getting rid of excessive shyness is daily and hard work. Unfortunately, psychological problems are not treated with pills and potions. A person will have not only to recognize its presence but also conduct serious work on himself, regardless of whether their indecision is inborn or acquired. It is better to "work out" shyness with a specialist in getting rid of fears and addictions.

This will allow you to get the desired result much faster. It's not all about only advice and conduct sessions during which we determine the reasons for the behavior and look for ways to solve the problem, but also ask them to follow the recommendations in everyday life. I am ready to share them with you:

Visualization is an integral part of the study of any problem. Often imagine yourself cheerful, confident, and liberated.

Shyness and restraint usually appear when a person mentally "tries on" certain ideals. Try to determine what it is, your standard, a comparison with which brings you into such a state. Remember where this collective image came from (I'm sure that it is collective, since usually people give it an unrealistic amount of positive qualities, and you and I are not perfect, as you know).

Why do you constantly compare yourself with this ideal? Answer this question. Do you think about it? That's great! And now we are trying to forget about the standards and perceive ourselves as you are.

Write your positive and negative qualities on a piece of paper. Think about which of the "minuses" you do not like the most. Is this such a terrible flaw that must be so securely hidden from prying eyes? Really no? Accept this trait of your character and do not be afraid to open it to others.

It will be difficult to do this right away, so I suggest that you first "train" mentally, and then gradually transfer to reality.

Learning to look at yourself from the outside without judgment and judgment is difficult. But those who want to forget about shyness forever will have to do it. Neutral vision will help awaken positive emotions. A feeling of joy, love for others, and yourself will be manifested.

Now attention! We take this same love and direct it to that trait of your character that you do not like and are trying to hide from others. Having done this simple manipulation, you will understand that in fact, everything is not so bad, and you have absolutely nothing to hide.

Remember that humor must always be present in our lives. But do not confuse him with sarcasm! Make fun of your indecision and timidity. Do not judge yourself for these qualities. Take them as an excuse to engage in self-development and self-improvement.

Also remember the cases when you felt confident in a company, in front of an audience, at work. Try to relive the positive emotions that you then experienced mentally. Imagine how you collect them into one great sense of faith in yourself, and "give yourself the setting" for its further development.

Try to observe the deeply hidden energy blocks that make you feel insecure and constricted. If you are unable to cope with this task, do not worry. Together we will work on this issue, and destroy the invisible wall, replacing it with confidence in our abilities and actions.

In your environment, there are liberated people who are constantly in the spotlight, and how do a magnet attract others? Observe their behavior. Perhaps you can figure out the secret to their success. Try comparing yourself with them and see if you have similarities. Notice the resemblance? Fine! Develop these qualities, and they will help you become more confident in yourself and look at the world with different eyes.

For some people, it is recommended to try to act like their standards of freedom and enslavement. But this must be done very carefully so as not to cross that thin line that will lead to simple imitation, and this is not our goal.

Learn to relax. Meditation and yoga will help strengthen your spirit.

Learn to mentally put an energy shield (imagine that it is made of confidence and positive emotions). This will help protect yourself from negativity.

It will be advisable you surround yourself with positive people, instead of thinking about how you look and how others evaluate you, you pay more attention to people who are nearby, to what and how they say, listen carefully. Show your sincere participation. And your attention will surely move away from any form clumsiness and awkwardness towards the dignity of other people. And, of course, people feel and appreciate it.

However, not only shy, is inclined to be silent. It has been researched that silence is one of the probable reactions that we feel in certain situations. But due to the fact that shy people do not manage to express themselves over and over again, they are less able to create their inner world. When people communicate with each other, they bargain and make deals - regarding mutual obligations, services, time, personal security, love, etc. Life is like a used goods store where everything can be purchased at a reasonable price.

Excessive shyness can bring us a lot of trouble. Most people say that when they get rid of it, they feel updated by "newly born" people. Some of them, after study, began to climb the career ladder successfully, but for some, it was an impetus for building relationships. Believe me. Nothing is impossible in life!

It should be noted that shyness can prevent a person from achieving their goals and living a full life. Sometimes it is better to admit your shyness openly, there are outwardly shy people and inwardly shy people. Outwardly shy people blush, stammer, get confused in speech, nervously tug on clothes, etc.

While Internally shy people may seem calm and unperturbed externally, but internally they are scared and tense. Often internally shy people are mistaken for arrogant or unfriendly, which is far from the truth.

Outwardly shy people, it is better to admit their shyness directly, as this is already obvious. This will help people who communicate with you not to pretend that they do not notice your shyness and not feel embarrassed because you do not look into their eyes, blush, etc.

When you confess your shyness, you let people know that you want to communicate, you want to be part of a group. It helps people around you feel more comfortable with you.

As for the internally shy people who outwardly look quite confident in themselves, there are situations when it is better not to speak openly about your shyness. For example, if you are at an important business meeting, or you know that your interlocutors can use your recognition to the detriment of you (gossip, manipulation, etc.).

The purpose of openly recognizing your shyness is not to enlist the approval of others, but to explain to them why you are behaving like this (do not look into the eyes, pull your sleeves, be silent, etc.) so that they do not feel uncomfortable nearby with you. During the conversation, try to contribute to the communication, do not be silent all the time, do not shift the entire burden of communication on the shoulders of the interlocutor.

I hope that my simple steps will help you overcome the difficulties. Of course, this is not a "recipe for happiness," but they will be able to simplify your life to overcome anxiety greatly.

3.5 Know Yourself

Each person has a certain set of desires, goals, and dreams. However, very often these desires and goals are false due to anxiety and they are also imposed by society, parents, friends or other authorities which is the major reason why you need to know more about yourself.

What does it mean to know oneself? To look at yourself from the outside, look into yourself, in your so-called deep inner world, see all this as it really is - is this to know yourself?

Many people confuse the knowledge of oneself with the vision of oneself, believing that to see something is to know. Such people look at themselves (with different types of vision) and think that by doing so, they recognize themselves.

Well, a man will look at himself, so what? What can you see in yourself? The whole world? The whole universe? No one argues with the fact that man contains the whole world and the whole universe. But to see the whole World in oneself is NOT to know oneself.

To see oneself and to know oneself is not the same thing. Looking at yourself in a mirror hanging on the wall, or looking at the mirror of your soul, analyzing your psychic needs is nothing more than seeing yourself. In any case, all this will be nothing more than a reflection of a person in various mirrors, and not the person himself. But to see your reflection (physical, mental, and psychic) is NOT to know yourself.

The mirrors that I mentioned above give a person the opportunity to see himself. You need to see yourself before you begin to know, but you should not stop there, believing that what you see means knowledge. The saddest thing is that a person cannot fully see himself. Both physical and psychic vision does not allow a person to see everything in full. In any mirrors, only a part is reflected.

Reflection is always apart. And even more so if a person is reflected in this or that mirror. Man is too big even for his sight, both physical and psychic. A person's body, his soul (emotional state), his spirit (ideas, dreams,) are not fully seen by man, but only in parts. A person is able to see only a small part of his body, only some emotions experienced, as a rule, at the moment, and some ideas and dreams that are most important at the moment. That's all that a person can see by looking at himself.

But with regard to self-knowledge, then everything is different. If a person cannot see himself in full, then a person is capable of knowing himself in full. And this despite the fact that people are constantly changing.

How important is it for a person to see himself and how important is it for a person to know himself? Seeing yourself is important in order not to scare yourself with other people. This also applies to the appearance of man and his inner world. Perhaps that is why there is no need to see yourself completely, but only to the extent that other people see you. But to know oneself is necessary in order not to frighten oneself.

So, we found out that by looking in the mirrors (both hanging on the walls, and in the mirrors of one's soul, and psychic mirrors) a person is able to see himself for who he is. Now let's talk about what needs to be done in order to know ourselves. And for this, you need to be a creator. Self-knowledge of oneself is possible only in creativity. No creativity - no knowledge of oneself.

It's not just some kind of things that a person does every day, but it is a creativity that allows a person to know himself. Only being a creator can one know oneself, and otherwise, there is no one to know, and there is no reason to.

3.6 Panic Attack

A panic attack is a sudden attack of anxiety, which can result in both falling into a swoon, and a real tantrum. Usually, it begins in stressful moments for the body - for example, when you ride the subway in the heat or find yourself in a stuffy crowd.

As the name implies, the main symptom of a panic attack is a sudden and, seemingly, wanton attack of anxiety and fear. It is accompanied by unpleasant sensations: palpitations, a rush of cold sweat, trembling in the legs, chest pain, difficulty breathing, and so on. Symptoms can be very different, but the main thing is that they should pass without a trace in 5–20 minutes together with a feeling of fear. The diagnosis of a panic attack cannot be made solely on the basis of symptoms: it is necessary to make sure, that the cause of the symptoms is not any other disease (e.g., pathology of the heart).

A panic attack alone does not usually do any harm. Symptoms are extremely unpleasant but pass quickly enough. The main trouble getting the fear, the panic again: for example, for a person, a couple of times has experienced a panic attack in the subway, back down into the subway can be a big problem. Such fear is " self-fulfilling": a person experiences stress, and under the influence of stress, a panic attack develops again. In severe cases, it can be formed agoraphobia - a condition, when almost any interaction with society causes bouts of fear and discomfort, and man is forced to spend his life locked up.

From the point of view of physiology, a panic attack is an unjustifiably harsh response of the nervous system to an external stimulus, which in reality is not at all dangerous. All of its symptoms are part of the "hit or run" defense mechanism, which works, say, when you meet a bear in the forest. In these cases, indeed, there is a reason to fear, and often the heartbeat enables faster run. However, for a not entirely clear reason, this mechanism sometimes works without a bear, that is, for no apparent reason.

This makes panic attacks related to vegetovascular dystonia, a disorder of the autonomic nervous system. Abroad, such a diagnosis is not widely used as he does not say anything about the cause of the disease, characterizing only its mechanism.

What to Do, If You Started a Panic Attack

At that time, when there is a panic attack, there is no way to analyze the reasons. But there are several ways that can help you deal with an attack:

Take a few breaths in any container. It can be a plastic cup or even a bag - just breathe calmly into it. So you can quickly stabilize your breathing and cope with panic.

Turn your attention to something external. For example, count columns at a metro station or buttons on a jacket of a passerby - any concentration on foreign objects will help you to come to your senses and again feel the connection with reality.

Stay where you are, or rather sit down. During a panic attack, try to limit your movements, sit down as much as possible and, as it were, "freeze." This method, like the previous one, helps to focus on the world around us, and not on our unpleasant sensations.

Talk to someone. Yes, it may, at first sight, seem strange, but the casual passer-by, to whom you ask for help, is able to help you with just their attention. Communication with another person will give a feeling of security and distract from an attack.

How to Prevent Panic Attacks?

Alas, the medicine does not know why these attacks occur, why and how to fight - it is rather a general recommendation, which, however, will help you avoid attacks in the future.

Do not lead a sedentary lifestyle. There is a scientific hypothesis, that the occurrence of attacks due to the lack of endorphins, which our body produces during exercise. Therefore, even light aerobic training and walking can significantly make your life easier.

Try not to be nervous. Yes, we know, that this recommendation sounds funny - well, how can you not be nervous, when life is difficult? But, only peace of mind and save you from panic attacks and other ailments.

Do not drink coffee or reduce its use. Caffeine in large quantities causes a rapid heartbeat and can trigger a panic attack at the most unexpected moment.

Be careful with alcohol. Alcoholic drinks, like any pathogens, can cause unexpected reactions of the body - including causing an attack.

Be careful with medication. Analyze, if a panic attack associated with taking a new drug? Sometimes drugs provoke attacks, so consult your doctor.

When Do You Really Need Help?

We have already found out that a single panic attack does not pose any particular risk, but sometimes the fear of its repetition introduces you into a vicious circle. If the attacks began to happen frequently and you already cannot cope with this myself, it is best to seek medical attention, when the consequences were not too serious. In those cases, when there is a permanent panic attack, the use of special breathing techniques, psychotherapy, and antidepressants. Of course, all this happens under the supervision of a specialist - one cannot joke with health.

A panic attack is definitely surmountable! Strategically, you need to take a full course of psychotherapy. The cognitive-behavioral direction of psychotherapy is recognized as the most effective in world practice for such disorders. Tactically, antidepressants with an anti-anxiety effect and tranquilizers can be used for situational relief of an attack of panic, anxiety or fear.

However, it should be understood that in most cases, medicines will act only as a "crutch" and a temporary outlet, they are not able to change your attitude and the habit of scaring yourself already formed at the level of complex reflexes. Behind a variety of external symptoms, your fear of death and the anxiety of losing control require more thoughtful analysis and in-depth study and transformation of your existing relationship system.

3.7 Don't Get Bogged Down On Yourself

When we are in a social situation that makes us nervous, many of us tend to get bogged down in our anxious thoughts and feelings.

With personalization, for some reason, we begin to think that everyone present is watching and judging us. Attention is focused on bodily sensations - a person hopes that if he does this, he will be able to control himself better. But this excessive focus makes it even clearer to understand how nervous he is, causing more concern. It also makes it difficult to focus on talking and interacting with other people.

As soon as you move the focus from internal to external, a miracle happens - anxiety decreases. The more attention that is going on around you, the less anxiety.

Focus your attention on people. But not on what they think of you! Instead, do your best to establish a genuine connection with them.

You have to understand that anxiety is not something that can be easily identified as you think. Even if people notice that you are nervous, they will not think badly of you. Most likely, they will even be more tactful. Actually, listen to what is being said. Do not pay attention to your negative thoughts; just conduct a dialogue and fully participate in it.

Focus on the present instead of thinking about what you say in a minute. Stop desperate to be perfect - and you will weaken the internal pressure. Be genuine and real.

3.8 Learn to Control Your Breathing

A lot of changes happen in a person's body when he starts to worry. One of the very first symptoms is rapid breathing. This leads to physical symptoms of anxiety, such as dizziness, suffocation, increased heart rate, and muscle tension.

You need to develop the habit of slowing your breathing in the first seconds of anxiety. This will help to avoid the manifestation of his other physical symptoms. Practice the following exercise in a calm situation:

Sit comfortably, straighten your shoulders. Direct one of your hand on your chest and the second hand on your stomach. Calmly Inhale and through the nose for at least four seconds. The hand on the stomach should rise, and the hand on the chest should be practically motionless. Hold your breath for at least two seconds.

Exhale slowly for six seconds, completely expelling air. As with inhalation, the hand on the stomach should lower down, and the hand on the chest should be motionless. Repeat this cycle ten more times.

3.9 Face Your Fears

The habit of avoiding anxiety situations can only exacerbate the problem, so you must overcome social anxiety by directly dealing with what causes fear (but there are also those who advise you to avoid this, so it all depends on the intensity of the emotions experienced under this kind of stress) Ask yourself honestly: the stronger and more desperate to avoid something, the worse it will become, right? And from here to the phobia at hand.

Avoidance is also harmful because it can interfere with many goals. For example, the fear of communication with people will prevent you from standing out, promoting your ideas, and simply will not allow you to make friends. Overcoming social anxiety may seem impossible, but it is quite realistic if you take it one step at a time (one of the most effective treatments for any phobia). The essence of this approach is to start with an easy task that does not cause discomfort, and gradually complicate it, moving up the "ladder of eradicating social anxiety."

Suppose, for example, that you are afraid to interact with colleagues. Let's build our staircase:

Step one: say hello to all your colleagues.

Step two: ask your colleagues for advice on your work.

Step Three: Ask your colleagues about how they spent the weekend.

Step Four: Talk with colleagues during lunch about the weather or football.

Step Five: Invite a colleague for coffee after work.

Of course, you can start right away with the fifth step, which seems quite reasonable, but the fact is that logic and rational, in this case, do not work. A man is afraid of everything, although he understands that he is cowardly. Therefore, use the "ladder to eradicate anxiety" and start small.

Make an Effort to Socialize

The key to success in curing social anxiety is action. Even if they drag you into events by force, nothing will change without your conscious participation. Sign up for any courses: yoga, meditation, chess, intellectual club. This will allow one way or another to interact and meet new people.

Also, develop your communication skills. Attend seminars, read books, and take online courses. This will help you become fully interested in the art of communications and realize how interesting this area of life is.

Choose Life Without Stress

Now let's talk about physiology. When you start to change it, you will automatically begin to get rid of stress. What causes stress when it comes to physiology? Lack of sleep, malnutrition, alcohol consumption, smoking, sedentary lifestyle. This means that you need to act in exactly the opposite way - after a few weeks, you can almost effortlessly cope with your psyche in social situations, especially if you listen to other tips.

Of course, if you feel that you have developed a social anxiety, be sure to contact a specialist. However, nothing prevents you from taking into account the recommendations that I gave in this chapter.

CONCLUSION

Do you feel anxious? I asked this question to so many people, and most of them looked at me, smiled, and answered:

Is this a rhetorical question? Naturally, we are all anxious. Maybe you're not anxious?

And then I found myself in a difficult position: when I asked this question to myself, I realized that I also have a feeling of anxiety. We are all anxious. And now, before now, I was anxious and thought if I could say what I needed. Yes, and I'm anxious.

You go to school and see small children - it turns out, and they have tension, race, panic, and insecurity in their lives. Yes, we are all anxious. Incredibly, it has become a global epidemic. We are all in this state.

The most unpleasant thing is that anxiety is something that cannot be described; you do not know what it is. You try to find the words - and you 'can't. What is this, after all? This is a fear-overwhelming soul, insecurity, a sense of impending disaster, or painful memory of what has already happened. So we live: either we are afraid of what might happen, or what has already happened does not let go, confuses and oppresses us internally, without leaving our mind alone for a minute.

We are always in a hurry somewhere; we do not know how to enjoy life. We are constantly in pursuit, constantly waiting for something new, different from what we have today. And the question arises: when will we rejoice today? When will we enjoy it? After all, what is here and now, in your hands, disappears so quickly.

Time flies. I say, the present constantly eludes us, we constantly live in another time - between the past and the future - and do not notice the present. Now the clock shows the beginning of the second, but we do not live this hour, but tomorrow or the day after tomorrow, we think about what will happen in a month, what we will be. And we look into the future, not creatively, but with a sense of anxiety.

For example, now you are doing some kind of work that pleases you, but a little later it will cease to please you because you will begin to think about the following tasks, and then about the next, and so on. We never live today, we do not live here and now - and yet this is the only reliable and safe.

This is what belongs to you so that you can enjoy the greatest gift of life. Nevertheless, anxiety does not leave us, and we are rushing between what happened in the past, between memories, experiences, events, and what could theoretically happen in the future.

Thus, life goes by, years fly by, and we become ill. We are not happy, we are not enjoying, we have troubled faces, troubled hearts, we cannot smile, we cannot understand what is happening and we cannot stop. It becomes scary if you think about where we are in such a hurry.

For many people, it is desirable to have a life in the midst of society or for some, even in the limelight. On the other hand, there is an increasing number of people suffering from social anxiety. For many people, it is increasingly difficult to participate in social life.

The constant fear of doing something wrong in everyday social contact robs much of their quality of life. The social anxiety is therefore associated with a strong avoidance behavior; untreated, this, in turn, leads to social isolation.

When becoming acquainted with new people or engaging in a public activity becomes a burden, the step towards isolation is not far away. The fear of everyday things in public, such as shopping or withdrawing money, paralyzes, and makes those affected feel stress.

Once in isolation, the way back on its own is difficult and hard to cope without professional help. Social anxiety is one of the most prominent anxiety disorders.

The biggest fear of people with social anxiety is strangely, embarrassingly, or even ridiculously felt by other people. Their behavior and visible signs of their fear are embarrassing. These include blushing, sweating, or shaking. Anxiety refers to situations in which you, as a person, maybe the focus of attention, observation, or evaluation.

It can also occur in situations where contact with other people becomes necessary, such as conversations with strangers, with people of the opposite sex, or when dealing with authority figures. Situations like these avoid people with social anxiety as much as possible or only keep them under a lot of fear. An increase in physical anxiety reaction can range to a panic attack.

Social anxiety reduces the quality of life and is a serious mental illness that should be treated under professional supervision. The goal of the different forms of therapy in social anxiety is always the same: the overcoming of one's sense of shame and the strengthening of one's sense of self. This includes the confrontation with problematic everyday situations in the middle of society. Anxiety and panic disorders can be treated well with a variety of psychotherapeutic approaches, as highlighted in previous chapters of this book. Hence, lasting and significant improvement in the quality of life is possible - the first step, however, must be taken by those affected. So that intense anxiety symptoms such as stress, sweating, blushing, and trembling soon no longer dominate everyday life.

CPSIA information can be obtained
at www.ICGtesting.com
Printed in the USA
LVHW011142111119
636963LV00002B/531/P